THE RED AND THE

A PORTRAIT OF ʻ

GERARD CAIRNS

ISBN

978-1-5272-1558-0

Acknowledgements

This has been a very personal portrait of a man I have researched, studied, lectured on, debated and written about for a long time. It has been a pleasure to research and write this particular work.

No book can be written in isolation. I am indebted to my long-time friend and comrade, Donald Anderson for allowing me to dip into his wealth of knowledge on Scottish history in general and John MacLean in particular. I got to meet Nan Milton through Donald which was a fine experience for a, then, young socialist. I am also very grateful to Eddi Reader, the superb singer and interpreter of song. Eddi very kindly made some material accessible from her great Uncle Seumas Reader's archive which included original articles from MacLean's Vanguard newspaper and information that helps to piece together a jigsaw that links MacLean to the Emerald Isle. Thanks must also go to Stephen Coyle, researcher and writer, for making sense of Irish politics in Scotland. A big thanks also to Jim Glass for use of a personal, signed photo of John which adorns the front cover and to Jim Clayson, a fine researcher who passed on some gems that he discovered. I am also grateful to the staff of the National Library of Scotland and the Public Records Office in Edinburgh and the Mitchell Library in Glasgow as well as to Audrey Canning and the Gallacher Memorial Library at Glasgow Caledonian University It was great to receive a testimonial from Jim McLean who helped give us a folk revival here in Scotland.

In cyber space I am grateful to the Marxists.org and Scottish Republican Socialist Movement websites which are both treasure troves of information from making obscure articles and pamphlets available to great photographs too. I have acknowledged them in the book as I go.

I must also acknowledge those no longer with us. To past Convenors of the John MacLean Society, Bill Johnston and

Jim Young, who taught me lots about the Left in times gone by. Some will remember a lovely, eccentric, wee man called Jimmy Wilson who shared a name with one of the executed Scottish Radicals of 1820 and who used to always regale 1820 Society commemorations with one of the worst political songs you will ever hear called "Scotland Free." He taught me an invaluable lesson about 'isms' and their bankruptcy. I was too young to appreciate it then but I remember well his words and message.

Finally, to my wee Granny Cairns. Annie introduced me to John MacLean and his heroics. "A good man" she told me and she introduced me to Scotland, Ireland and the Social Revolution before John MacLean did!

A h-uile duine, tha mi fada, fada nur comainn!

GC

September 2017

For Shirley and Lucy, my wife and my daughter whose love and support make everything possible.

Author's Note

This journey has taken me from Pollokshaws to Stornoway
via Edinburgh. My intention is to paint a picture of
John MacLean in words. I am not seeking to compete with
the classic biographies by Nan Milton and John Broom. It
may not even be proper biography but it is my pen
portrait of John MacLean.

I have consulted some Gaelic sources. I am an adult
learner who is by no means fluent but have tried to stay
true to the language and have given the language its
place in so far as original quotes in Gaelic I have kept
in Gaelic with my English language translation in the
footnote.

I was the last Secretary of the John MacLean Society.
Hopefully someone else will be inspired to carry on a
fine tradition.

Contents

THE RED AND THE GREEN –

A PORTRAIT OF JOHN MACLEAN

Introduction

CLANN MACGILL-EAIN

Chan e iadsan a bhàsaich

Ann an àrdan Inbhir-Chèitein,

Dh' aindeoin gaisge is uabhair,

Ceann uachdrach ar sgeula;

Ach esan bha 'n Glaschu

Ursann-chatha nam feumach,

Iain mòr MacGill-Eain,

Ceann is fèitheam ar sgeula.

    - Sorley MacLean (1)

In Glasgow it looked like your average Saturday Evening Times. The football was on the front. My team, St Mirren, had beaten Motherwell 2 - 0. That caught my attention. It is a little known fact about the Red Clydesider, John MacLean, that he liked the football too. His team was Queens Park and their result was there too: a nil - nil draw with Clyde. (2)

He didn't know that because he was also on the front page. The headline read simply: "John MacLean dead." He had died the day before on St Andrews day and they got his age wrong stating that he was fifty. He was in fact only 44 years of age.

By the Monday there was more detail as the burial had happened in Pollokshaws led by the Clyde Workers Silver Band. Tom Anderson led the indoor, secular service although there was a minister present, Reverent Richard Lee, with members of the "Republican Party." The Band played the Death March from *Saul*. 3000 lined the streets to pay their respects. (3) Anecdotal accounts put that figure closer to 10000. The paper also reported Tom Johnston, who would be a future Secretary of State for Scotland, visiting to view the remains. There is a classic photograph of the cameraman on top of the van filming the funeral and it is an interesting topic of conversation among those interested in MacLean and the Red Clydeside period as to what happened to that footage. It was shown at some John MacLean commemorations.in the 1930's (4)

It was good that Glasgow's local paper paid a wee tribute. Her sister - the arch Tory Glasgow Herald - didn't mention his passing as far as I could see.

This all happened in 1923. 91 years later the land of his birth would host the Commonwealth Games and a referendum on Independence. As a participant and a firm Yes supporter I took a keen interest in the Referendum debate. None of the mainstream Left of Centre parties mentioned this icon of the Left. Yet beamed out to millions worldwide, a young South African singer - Pumeza Matshikiza - sang Hamish Henderson's *Freedom Come All Ye* with the line:

"When MacLean meets wi' his freends in Springburn..."

Very few would have seen the significance; some would not have known the reference. Hamish Henderson did and enshrined John MacLean in his great song of peace and internationalism in the Scots tongue. MacLean in Glasgow working to make his city, his country, his world better. No other individual gets a mention - just John MacLean.

This book is part a personal labour of love but also to position John MacLean in terms of history, politics and culture. The definitive biography will always be Nan Milton's *John MacLean*. I will reference the others as well as the primary sources, pamphlets and songs and poems written about him. I will try and give his politics a context, a positioning and some observations that are rooted in the human as well as the ideology. MacLean would not approve as he was a Marxist pure and simple. It was all for the cause and the cause was human.

His politics are fascinating of course. The book is in 2 parts that look at his life as a principled, socialist opponent of the First World War and educator and the impact of national identity on his politics through the prism of Ireland. He was a truly remarkable, carnaptious, passionate man who wanted to make a difference to this planet and the MacLean that Ms Matshikiza sang about does not deserve to become a footnote in history.

He was also a husband and a dad. This will be acknowledged too as it is the humanity that matters. Humanity made him oppose capitalism and War. Humanity made him sacrifice. Humanity made him want for the world what he wanted for Scotland. He was a truly warm, complex human being just like you and me I suppose.

NOTES

(1)   TS Law and Thurso Berwick (eds) *Homage to John MacLean*, 1973. It was first published in 1943.
Translation from the Gaelic:
Clan MacLean

Not they who died
In the hauteur of Inverkeithing,
In spite of valour and pride,
The high head of our story,
But he who was in Glasgow
The battle post of the poor,
Great John MacLean,
The top and hem of our story.
(2)   Glasgow Evening Times, 1/12/1923.
(3)   Ibid, 3/12/1923.
(4)   Comrade Tom (Anderson), *Comrade John MacLean, MA*, 1930.

PART 1 - "The Socialist Army."

We need technicians' not great men or admirable men.
Technicians specialised in the liberation of the masses,
licensed demolition experts who will have scorn for the
idea of personal escapism because their work will be
their life.

- Victor Serge (1)

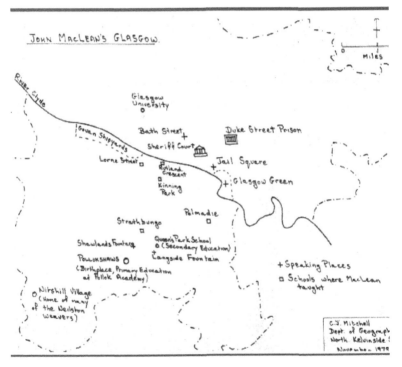

A teaching aid used in North Kelvinside primary by one
of the teaching staff, CJ Mitchell given to the author
by Donald Anderson, another fine socialist Dominie.

Chapter 1 - The Convert

XI - The philosophers have only interpreted the world, in various ways; the point, however, is to change it.

- Karl Marx (2)

Sometimes it is easy to pinpoint the time when your life has changed forever. For John MacLean it was when he discovered Karl Marx. There is no doubting there is something inspirational about the German philosopher. The wild hair, the big beard and a writing style that was, is sensational with a real journalistic pace and political passion.

With his lifelong friend and colleague, Frederick Engels, he published some of the most influential left wing literature and propaganda. Charlie and Freddie were quite a double act and between them they were able to articulate the class struggle into a theory of history and sought to articulate socialism as a science. Charlie on his own gave us the great critique of capitalism - *Capital* or *Das Kapital* in its original German. It wasn't enough to see that the working class were living in slums and suffering from mass poverty and disease. You can always close your eyes. No, there was a theory as to why this was happening; a theory of expropriation; a theory from extensive research of other economists as to how capitalism worked and why it worked that way. The future of that system could be predicted.

The working class were so important that he called them by a special name - the proletariat. This term came from the Latin, proletarius, or class of wage earners. These proletarians would not just liberate themselves but humanity.

Everything about his writing and theorising was different.

A young man from Pollokshaws in Glasgow (although outside the boundaries back then) took heed and converted. This young man was a MacLean of Highland descent. He was born on the 24th August 1879, the sixth child of Daniel MacLean and Anne MacPhee. The Highland Clearances had led both of them away from the Gàidhealtachd to the west of Scotland. Daniel was a Maclean from Mull where the clan had traditionally resided and where their castle, Duart, still dominates the coastline. John's mother, Anne, came from Corpach at the foot of Ben Nevis. MacLean never forgot this heritage. At his trial in May 1918 for sedition against World War 1 he ascribed his fidelity to the working class, "because my people were swept out of the Highlands." (3) MacLean never forgot this.

Tom Anderson, in the first biography of MacLean, attributes John's looks to his mother:

"His mother, whom I had the pleasure of meeting, was a woman with a great personality. As I see her now I see John – the same face, the same head, the same merry twinkle in the eye, the same quick impulse, the same in height and build." (4)

Both parents had the Gaelic and it was spoken at home but as with most Gaelic-speaking parents, it was believed that the imperial tongue was the language of progress. There is no evidence that John spoke Gaelic. However, the MacLean's were brought up as Free Church or 'Wee Frees' to the uninitiated. They differed from the Free Presbyterian Church who were the real Wee Frees. This was the Church that broke away from the Church of Scotland during the great Disruption of 1843 although the MacLeans belonged to the Original Secession Church which had actually broken away 21 years earlier but had merged in with the Free Church by the time of John's birth. John would later say that the difference between the Wee Frees and the United Frees was a difference over property rights. They had a strong base in the Highlands and Islands and were more austere in their faith, Gaelic played a large part and it is possible that the young John would have heard Gaelic psalms - he may even have known some - in their unique, precented form. This is a very hypnotic style of singing which is at times both beautiful and harrowing to these Catholic ears.

The Original Secession Church, Pollokshaws

Mum was a nurse and Dad was a labourer. In true working class fashion, Daniel died young. He was only 43 when he died in 1888. John would be only a year older when he passed away in 1923. Anne worked hard to ensure that her family got their education and both John and one of his brother's, Daniel junior, trained to be teachers. After leaving school, he became a trainee teacher at Polmadie

School and went to the Free Church Training College when he was 19. He could have been a strict, Calvinist teacher but for a different set of circumstances. He was also studying for his Master of Arts at Glasgow University.

John would discover Marx and reject his faith. His own daughter Nan and Tom Anderson have their own take on Christian hypocrisy at that time affecting him while John Broom argued that it was the debates that he had in the Secession Church that convinced him that religion meant nothing. There is no reason to doubt this but it is also true that too many scholars of MacLean ignore the influence that religion had on him: on his sense of morality; his single mindedness of purpose and belief that came out at various times in his life. Nan tells the story of how a friend called Daniel MacDougall ran a character album and MacLean's interview revealed his favourite authors as, "Marx, Blatchford, Shelley" and his heroes as, "John Ball, Socrates, Jesus." (5) He had a favourite painter but no favourite composer. Music didn't rock his boat.

The gentle Christ still played a part in inspiring MacLean while his Churches didn't. As we say iin the west of Scotland about a lot of things you could take the boy out a Presbyterian Church but you couldn't take the Presbyterian out the boy. The cultural influences are revealing too - they are mostly English inspired. In the cultural colony of England that was Scotland, it would take a lot of digging and education to find some Scottish cultural references. For this reason, MacLean thought nothing of it when he picked up Robert Blatchford's *Merrie England* to supplement his reading of *Capital.* It was expected reading for a Social Democrat.

A Young John (standing) with some friends.

His rejection of Calvinism led him into a local
ecumenical organisation called the Progressive Union.
This was a debating club that allowed local rebels to
come together to discuss the finer points of socialism,
anarchism, philosophy and it would not be long before
MacLean was looking for an organisation that expressed
his views. The good people of Pollokshaws picked up
their local paper on a September morning in 1902 to hear
the case for the class struggle:

"That the class struggle is bitter, we need only reckon
the annual death toll of the workers, the maimed, the
poisoned, the physically wrecked by overwork, the

mentally wrecked by worry, and those forced to suicide through desperation. It is a more bloody and more disastrous warfare than that to which the soldier is used. Living in slums, breathing poisonous and carbon loaded air, wearing shoddy clothes, eating adulterated and life-extinguishing food, the workers have greater cause for a forcible revolution than had the French capitalists in 1789." (6)

MacLean had joined the Socialist Army. He wasn't advocating violence but rather that workers should carry, "the class struggle into the political field." This was his Army's methodology. The cause was the cause of the Social Democracy and it was no surprise that a year later MacLean joined the Social Democratic Federation (SDF.) This group had been formed in 1884 by Henry Hyndman who had a right wing past and whose British patriotism didn't go away. Yet this was the home for Marxists of that generation. Social Democratic parties had sprung up all over Europe.

The newspaper of the SDF was *Justice*. In its first issue in January 1884 its 12-point programme is emblazoned at the top of the page. There are some demands that hark back to the Chartist era; democratic reforms such as Federalism and the abolition of the Lords; "legislative" independence for Ireland; land nationalisation; separation of Church and State. (7) Socialism is not mentioned once. Yet the editorial signed by Hyndman, William Morris and J Taylor is an impassioned plea for, "organised Socialism in the British Islands."

Marx had died the year before. The success of the Bolsheviks in Russia in 1917 have led many modern Marxists to be highly critical of the Social Democratic parties focussing on their gradualism, their turning away from Marx's revolutionary message and finally their capitulation in 1914 to their national governments and abandonment of the Socialist International.

There is a counter argument in terms of what the Social Democracy meant. These were classical Marxists who talked the language of the great Cooperative Commonwealth, of the importance of working class education and of laying building blocks for a genuine socialist democracy. Human beings contributed to its failure for a whole host of reasons. For me the first principles of the Social Democracy were rooted in the cause of human liberation and it is worthwhile to remember it. (8)

MacLean embraced the Party and became heavily involved in its organisation in Pollokshaws and in time across Scotland. His real niche would soon come to the fore. His oratory and his grasp of Marxian theory as well as his ability to disseminate it as a teacher would mark John MacLean out from the rest of the crowd. The influence of Charlie Marx was all over MacLean's early writings in *Justice* and his letters to the Independent Labour Party's ILP) paper, *Forward*.

MacLean's early writings show a passionate young man who appreciated the building blocks. He had studied how capitalism works like his mentor but he was not repeating mantras in a parrot like fashion:

"Whilst the laws of capitalist production discovered by Marx form the foundation of our beliefs and actions, yet they have only become deep convictions as a consequence of using our own eyes and brains." (9)

His eye and brain saw in Pollokshaws and Glasgow what Charlie and Freddie saw in the slums of Manchester. The scale might have been different but the root cause was the same - capitalism and exploitation and this meant that through Marx was the route to a socialist society:

"It therefore becomes a duty for every socialist to comprehend Marxian principles because only by scientific knowledge can we know our social surroundings, can we explain social evolution and, therefore, efficiently and speedily accomplish the social transformation (ie the social revolution) necessary to the establishment of socialism." (10)

Duty; knowledge; explain; necessary. Not only words but building blocks. The building blocks are there and they mark out his Social Democratic Party from the others on the Left primarily the reformist Labour Party. Perhaps it wasn't, isn't and never will be a science but the enablers are there that will lead to the Promised Land. This was not MacLean's view. Socialism was science as well as his new faith. To emphasise his break from Christianity the new way was spelled out in the same article:

"Capitalism is forging ahead at a terrific rate, and at an increasing rate; society is evolving at an unprecedented pace. Surely, then, we socialists cannot afford to grope; we must lead not follow capitalism. To that end we must have special scientific knowledge in our own lines of business; we must have half an hour's experiments every day in school for our children, instead of trying to follow Paul on propaganda tours, or trying to parrot answers and inappropriate proofs to silly questions; and we must study Marx to know how best to lift society on to the higher evolution we are pleased to call socialism." (11)

If you know your Bible, as John did from his studies in the Free Church College, then Saul/Paul was also a convert. It took one to know one. MacLean would soon be on his own propaganda tours. In late 1907 he went on his first foray across the border to Carlisle at the invitation of the local SDF. He was becoming more polemical and got involved in a good old fashioned rammy with the Labour Party over the heart and soul of socialism in the pages of Forward over 1909-10.

These really were exciting times and there is a zeal for socialist change. At the turn of the century a bus toured London inscribed with the words: **Socialism – the only hope of the World!** MacLean never forgot these first principles and in a letter to Forward defended the SDP's 'dogmatic' approach because it should be the ILP's too and in echoing the London bus he wrote:

"We fight for nothing short of socialism because we believe that nothing short of that will save the workers…And, after all, extremity is a virtue." (12)

Throughout his short life MacLean never shied from being extreme. He was on the side of truth not popularity and it could lead him to the fringes. It is important to remember especially in the context of his later life and fall out with the Communist Party. Tom Bell tells the story of his behaviour at a Workers Educational Association conference in 1909. John moved a motion protesting against the murder of the anarchist, Francisco Ferrer, in Barcelona and his motion was rejected as outside the scope of the conference. MacLean, by his force of argument, convinced about 100 comrades to march to the Spanish Consulate but it was closed (it was a Saturday.) Undeterred the group held an outdoor meeting anyway. (13)

He also related to people. He was often seen, with Capital under his arm, listening to what working class people had to say. Around the same time, a Shetland Islander – Peter Jamieson – told Nan such a story. It was in Lerwick and Mr Jamieson was getting John up to speed on the 'iniquities of landlordism.' With his good book under his arm:

"He was most attentive and the tenderness of his heart was outstandingly apparent when there was mention of oppression and hardship." (14)

Such stories give a view of MacLean's Marxism. It was not an intellectual thing for him although he was certainly well read. John seldom in his writings makes reference to the philosophical writings of Marx or his musings on the great questions of his day. Capital was different. It was practical. It was a handbook that could let working class people understand how they were being exploited and the activist in him could give some answers; some education on what to do to end this rotten state of affairs. Charlie had to immerse himself in weighty tomes in a big London library to write his good book. MacLean never felt the need to base himself in a library and he didn't have to. He would take the message out with zeal to raise the banner of the great Social Democracy.

MacLean was certainly a loyal Social Democrat. All his campaigning reflected the party's activity which led him into campaigns. One of his first was on public health in Greenock which resulted in his first pamphlet, *The Greenock Jungle*. This was written in late 1907. It is no classic of socialist literature by any means although it was a campaigning tract in support of a fellow activist, James Houston, who had exposed some practices in the Greenock slaughter house. Amid the exposure of the scandal of cheap production methods and substandard food being sold was the Social Democratic message. It was perfectly logical that capitalists should behave this way. The scandal was not merely a Greenock scandal but had a message for all towns and cities in Britain:

"This exposure of the Beef Scandal of Greenock will have been useless unless it has added another to the many apparent facts of everyday life, proving that only when property is owned by the people and used by the people to create those things necessary for life and happiness, shall we have swept away for ever poverty, adulteration, and the multitude of the attendant evils of Capitalism. The only hope of the masses of mankind lies in Socialism. Individual initiative and incentive in the beef trade are bad for the people; social initiative and incentive alone make for justice." (15)

Socialism – the only hope of the world! It is truly inspiring to look back at socialist literature at this period and witness a passionate zeal and desire for a new society based on real values and not sound bites. This zeal and desire took him to the Singers factory at Clydebank where the mostly female staff were out on strike in 1911 and also saw an early surge of his republicanism as the Scottish conference in May 1911. A resolution was passed against the coronation of George

V. This loyal British socialist made no reference to his later Scottish republic but only to devolution of powers or Home Rule as part of the resolution that also supported full female suffrage and proportional representation.

It was also through his lecturing that he met Agnes. Annie Gordon recalls how John would often visit her branch of the SDF; the College SDF (for Stow College.) Annie was the daughter of an early socialist pioneer, Willie Nairn. She takes up the romantic tale:

"He was giving an outdoor lecture and this lady was standing, a young woman, and because was going round with literature, and because women so seldom stood at our meetings, I spoke to her and, apparently, her people had come from the same town as his people. I said to her, 'well why not wait and speak to him?', and so she did." (16)

Agnes Wood hailed from the Borders and they actually met when John was speaking in Hawick trying to form an SDF branch in 1907. This was her part of the world and I can only imagine that Annie Gordon was referring to Langside/Pollokshaws where they currently stayed. She worked as a nurse in the north of Glasgow. Annie Gordon cites Ruchill hospital while his daughter Nan cites Stobhill and both women were probably right as she was probably an itinerant nurse. John, or Johnnie to give him his pet name, started to make some more frequent visits to the hospital to woo her. He was human after all and even John MacLean took some days off from the great socialist cause but no doubt two socialists who fancied each other probably talked about the cause a lot. They struck a connection and were engaged at Christmas 1908 and married in December 1909. This would have given him as with all human beings a great lift to have some form of romance in his life and to have some emotional support in the sometimes lonely existence of travelling all over to lecture and agitate. John Broom gives examples of some of his letters to Agnes from his one and only Mediterranean cruise in the summer of 1909 where John and his friend James McNabb got to experience continental breakfasts in France and Italy as well as a visit to a Mosque in North Africa.

It wouldn't be long before they had a family. Two daughters - Jean and Agnes (or Nan.) born in 1911 and 1913 respectively. Mrs Agnes MacLean would subsume her own socialist politics into the duty, as it was perceived to be then, of being Mother and raising the girls. This was the inherent chauvinism in politics and political activism. Johnnie was the breadwinner as an employed teacher and the political struggle went on for him as usual.

Proud parents with baby Jean.

MacLean's support for the Cooperative Commonwealth or socialist republic led him to support the Cooperative movement for a short time from 1911 to about 1914. The principles of Cooperation went back to the mid nineteenth century and had played a strong part in the Labour movement. MacLean tried to take his first principles to some conferences notably in Perth and in Paisley. The message was simple; to build a truly cooperative society then the current capitalist form of society has to be overthrown. This message would have been too strong for many in the Movement at that time. In MacLean's reports of these conferences, however, we see MacLean talking about how the Social Democracy might look: by seizing control of the trusts and their stores, controlling them socially and uniting them at a local and national (and international) level then the seeds are being sown for a different type of society. (17) He didn't do enough of this but it was something.

In the pantheon of the Left there are many critiques of capitalism and many assertions of its replacement. Very few - not Marx nor MacLean - really go into what socialism would look or feel like. The Bolsheviks produced all sorts of rubbish about discipline and Party and democratic centralism but their inadequacies of theory and practice were shown up in power.

MacLean dipped his toes in this water. Like the rest he was stronger in condemning the existing order of society.

Perhaps this goes back to Charlie and Freddie. I remember Jim Young arguing that there were two Marxism's. The nineteenth century critique of capitalism and the twentieth century ideology. Revolutionaries of today like to go on about Russia. You can draw your own conclusions about the link between Marx and the Bolshevik/Stalinists and their version of a socialist society. MacLean's strength was to take the critique to a different level and educate the working class of central Scotland in the basics of Marxian economics. He

influenced that generation of socialists many of whom
would become career Labour politicians or Communist
party apparatchiks although, to be fair, not to be
careerists or apparatchiks. How was he to know? He
influenced left wing Scottish nationalists to explore
Marx and his teachings. (18) As well as young activists,
trade unionists and a young, beautiful woman who worked
in Ruchill hospital. John's conversion to Marxism shaped
him and his life and working class Scotland. It is the
starting point in his story.

Yet he could do these things because he was a gifted
teacher.

NOTES

1) Victor Serge, *Birth of our Power*, 1931, p.162

2) Karl Marx, Theses on Feuerbach, in *The Marx-Engels Reader*, 2nd edition (ed by Robert C Tucker), 1978, p.145

3) John MacLean, Speech from the Dock, 9 May, 1918, *In the Rapids of Revolution* (ed. Nan Milton), 1978, p. 111.

4) Comrade Tom (Anderson), *Comrade John MacLean, M.A.*, 1930 p.3.

5) Nan Milton, *John MacLean*, 1973, p. 23

6) Letter to the Pollokshaws News, 5/9/1902, in *In The Rapids of Revolution*, p.31

7) *Justice*, 19/1/1884

8) The late Jim Young insists that MacLean was a "classical Marxist" in his biography. See James D. Young, *John MacLean: Clydeside Socialist*, 1992, ch.3

9) John MacLean, Time-saving and Karl Marx, Justice, 14/12/1907, In the Rapids…p. 33

10) Ibid, p. 33

11) This quote is also from the same article but did not make Nan's edit in *In the Rapids*…This is taken from a fine collection edited by Will Johnson. John MacLean, *Essential Writings and Speeches*, nd, p. 14

12) John MacLean, *Why a Labour Party? Come out*! Forward, 30/7/1910 in MacLean, ibid. p. 37

13) Tom Bell, *John MacLean – A Fighter for Freedom*, 1944, p. 18

14) Milton, ibid, p.37

15) John MacLean, *The Greenock Jungle*, in *Essential Writings and Speeches* edited by Will Johnson, p.21

16) Annie Gordon talking to Michael Donnelly in 1967. This oral history was captured in Hugh Savage and Les Forster, All for the Cause – Willie Nairn, 1856 – 1902: Stonebreaker, Philosopher, Marxist. No date, p.61

17)   John MacLean, The Scottish Co-operative
       Conference, Forward,13/5/1911 in MacLean, ibid. p.
       62

18)   Ruaraidh Erskine of Mar in Guth na Bliadhna,
       An t-Earrach, 1921. Through MacLean's influence he
       explored Marx's writings in relation to the rural
       struggle for land.

Chapter 2 - Dominie

There was nane like John MacLean the fighting Dominie.

- Matt McGinn (1)

The professors in the universities claim to be impartial men of science. But nobody believes them. Their teaching has become a mere system of apologetics; by which they reveal the moral reasons that justify the plundering of the working class.

- John MacLean (2)

Dominie is a Scots word and in many ways it has become synonymous with John MacLean. He was a teacher in many, many more ways than by profession alone. True, he taught schoolchildren on the south side of Glasgow. He also taught socialists and working class activists and he was well into treble figures with the numbers of left wing adults he taught.

Being a teacher has so many negative connotations and yet, anecdotally, many people in working class communities remember their teacher. That said, the style, the content, the environment are not something that many people in my experience fondly reminisce about. I, however, loved school and had some teachers who were truly inspiring. Isn't that the purpose of education? To instill a thirst for learning that sets you up for life. It is certainly important to bear this in mind when we think of MacLean as the Dominie.

If teaching is more than a job and is really a vocation then MacLean exemplified this. Clydeside workers were certainly thirsty for more knowledge and MacLean's classes were unparalleled in Europe. It was truly his greatest contribution to the Socialist movement in Scotland at a practical level and we should not forget this.

Staff photo. Date/school unknown but John is second from left on the second row. (Source: the Mitchell Library papers.)

All praise goes to the old man with a big beard. No, not Charlie Marx but John Knox. MacLean was a product of the Calvinist educational tradition in Scotland. He attended the Free Church Teacher Training College from 1898 – 1900 and even though he abandoned his faith and became a convinced agnostic there was a relationship with Christianity all through his life.

There is the debate isn't there regarding organised Christianity versus Christ himself. MacLean would have read about the radicalism, the challenge to hypocrisy and that desire to make his apostles think for themselves through parable rather than telling them. Who learns by being told? (If you don't believe me how many times have you said, "he/she won't listen.") He would have studied the texts and it would not be lost on him the word of Mary Magdalene during the Resurrection story when she discovers who she is talking to - "rabonni." (3) The gentle Christ as teacher. The gentle Christ was in some ways an iconoclast too. Maybe that was why he was one of his heroes.

The young man from Pollokshaws came to reject the 'ism' but he didn't leave behind the ethics and the morality that he learned. In 1914 he summed this up succinctly in a way that displayed his hostility to the system. In a letter to the editor of Forward shortly after the outbreak of War he wrote:

"Capitalism has neither conscience nor morality when it is brought to bay." (4)

Conscience and morality mattered to him and would infuse his teaching. If MacLean was an iconoclast too, as his friend and fellow socialist Sylvia Pankhurst believed him to be, then his iconoclasm was genuine and rooted in two traditions:

"The iconoclast of iconoclasts, I have heard him in his hoarse voice with delighted smiles, expounding to his class on Marxian economics the parable of the three coats as though the very hearing of it were the universal cure-all, the true wine of life." (5)

It certainly proves the radical, Christian sub text to his teaching style and the language he used. Parables? True wine? Sylvia Pankhurst may have got her Biblical parables confused but the message is pertinent. Terry Brotherstone wrote disparagingly about how Christianity infused the Red Clydeside Labour MP's. Terry was a Trotskyist who wrote extensively about MacLean but Leon was his hero:

"The Scottish 'lefts', as Trotsky pointed out, were never so passionate as when they were defending in

parliament the property rights of the Scottish Church."
(6)

For Brotherstone, as a Marxist and an atheist, the
Scottish Labour MP's collectively were rooted in
religion and a moral view of socialism be it Wheatley
the Catholic MP for Shettleston, or the predominantly
Presbyterian Clydesiders. It is disparaging because it
fails to understand the cultural world that not only
they came out of but that MacLean came out of too. John
rejected his religion without any doubt but he could not
escape its cultural impact. It is more than fair to say
that Christ recurs in MacLean's speeches and reflections
throughout his life. For the Clydesiders it was God and
their faith which they held to as compatible with their
socialism which was certainly not the case with the
Marxist convert from Pollokshaws

Yet I believe that MacLean has to be considered in terms
of the influence of his abandoned faith no less than the
believing 'lefts.' Terry saw the religious baggage of
the Scottish left as a "gradualist disease" which is
just ultra-leftist rubbish. Many writers on MacLean
overlook his own formative, cultural influences
including Scottish Presbyterianism and would do well to
note that MacLean shared the same cultural traditions as
the other 'Scottish lefts.' He drew a different
conclusion. MacLean did not feel the need to publish a
pamphlet or a major article on his critique of organised
Christianity. Compare and contrast with James Connolly
across the water and there are many written musings on
the intertwining of Catholicism and Socialism and
national identity. John MacLean seemed a lot more
comfortable.

He did seem to retain an interest in the subject and
used his alias in the 'Gael' column in Justice to make
some observations primarily in relation to his old
Church. Indeed, his critique of organised religion on
behalf of the Social Democracy was a recurring theme
from 1911 - 14. This ranged from reports on United Free

Church general assemblies, the Church's attempts to organise "labour weeks" and other initiatives that we would now badge as social justice campaigns. MacLean was scathing of the Church and their hypocrisy as he saw it. In one such column he responds to the then Moderator's call for "man and women saturated with the faith and spirit of Christ" to attack the world's social problems:

> "We Social-Democrats know that the most
> bitter and unscrupulous attacks on us have
> come from saturated Christians. I do not
> blame Christ, remember, as he was neither
> Socialist nor Anti-Socialist. It is quite
> possible for charitable and soft-hearted
> Christians to harden their very hearts
> against us, not, because our principles are
> false or capitalism moral, but solely because
> we are called atheists. However they may try,
> such saturated Christians must fail in "good"
> work because their heads are muddled, and
> their standard of morality is antiquated. If
> saturated Christians wish to do good they
> must join our Party and fight with the faith
> and spirit of Socialists." (7)

His old hero from 1903, Christ, was not to blame which is worth pointing out. MacLean's Marxian critique of religion is usually glossed over with one line references to his Calvinist upbringing. I am not claiming for one second that he was something that he was not. He was an Agnostic in my opinion in the true sense of that term and not a believer unlike his socialist contemporaries on Clydeside. But he could not escape his old religion in terms of the influence it had on his formative years. Religion's failure of the working class and its justification of the prevailing

capitalist system necessitated a new morality, a higher
morality.

"If Socialists are striving for a world as an all-
inclusive co-operative human society, they surely are
advocates of the highest morality, as it would be the
rock foundation for the brotherhood and sisterhood of
all humanity." (8)

It was the language of the Reformer sounding thunder
against the old Church justifying the new order as the
higher moral code. For Gael, socialism was morally right
and just. I'm not sure if this is strictly Marxian but
remain to be convinced. Shortly before the outbreak of
War Gael devoted his column again to the United Free
Church. In contrasting the higher amount of socialist
clergy in England to the four ministers (all named) in
Scotland he reported on a speech by Reverend Dr. Reith
to the UF Assembly in Edinburgh on becoming Moderator.
The theme was poverty and the alienation of working
class people from the system and Gael quoted at length
from his speech and seemed impressed with the world view
of the new Moderator:

> "They must therefore maintain that the
> fundamental law of Christian ethics, brotherly
> love and mutual service; should be the basis
> on which our social system was to be
> reconstructed. When workers asked him why life
> should mean this for him and that for them, he
> had no answer to give that satisfied his own
> judgment, much less his conscience."

Gael sensed more than just platitudes. He praised a real
and genuine desire to attack injustice which he could
relate to as a Scottish socialist.

"Had the time not come for the Church, in the
name of Christ and humanity, to begin to insist
on the eradication of the cause which leads to
social evils A reunited Church of Scotland
should present itself in the eyes of their
fellow countrymen as one concentrated force,
bent, in Christ's name, on grappling with, and
ending the social sores from which our beloved
land suffered; bent on having His will done on
our own Scottish earth as it is done in heaven,
and on turning her wilderness into Eden." (9)

Gael felt that he had given the "gist" of Dr Reith's
address suggesting also that he 'got' Marx. Praise
indeed from this ex-believer and, as we shall see,
MacLean never lost this passion to take the great Social
Question to those in the Churches claiming to espouse
love, justice and peace to all.

So, the sub text alluded to is important and there are
two aspects to this. The first, obvious point is that
MacLean was a teacher. It was his job. He came out of
teacher training from the Free Church Teacher Training
College. He would have learned a methodology from which
he could hardly escape. This methodology stayed with him
all his life and probably explains his belief in
extremity being a virtue! One of the quirkier aspects is
the teacher training certificate from the Scotch
Education Department which gave him a 70% pass in
applying chalk to a chalk board! Secondly, John got his
degree in Political Economy from Glasgow University. I
think it is safe to say that he was proud of his degree
and it was a part of his personal identity as witnessed
by his signature: John MacLean, M.A. He served schools
on the south side of Glasgow most notably Kinning Park
and Govan. This provided for the new married couple
after 1909 when he married Agnes who hailed from Hawick.

He was on the career ladder to the extent that he became a deputy head teacher. Economics added to his methodology as it was practical and applicable to the world around him.

It is no mere accident or quirk that both Marxism and Education feature in some of his earlier writings. In 1908 the Liberal Government had published an Education Bill for Scotland. At the May Day rally, MacLean was instrumental in getting the "wage slaves of the land of Burns" to pass a resolution calling for an alternative Bill which called for:

"a) secular education; b) free maintenance of all school children; c) free books; d) extension of the age limit to 16 years; e) maintenance scholarships for all attending secondary schools, technical colleges and universities; f) free medical examination of all, with free treatment of such as require medical aid; g) the establishment of homes in the country and at the coast for the benefit of school children; h) all educational expenditure to be borne by the State." (10)

Like so many transformations in John's life, the First World War brought this crashing down. In 1915 amidst a heap of political activity the Govan School Board, as his employer, wanted to move him from Lambhill Street school to Lorne Street. MacLean objected to the move as well as to the lack of choice. He wrote to the Board on 29th June:

"The theory of the 'Divine Right of Kings' was, in the end, crushed and so will the Govan School Board's application of the 'Divine Right of Headmasters.'" (11)

John stuck to his guns and the relationship broke down fuelled no doubt by MacLean's short term of imprisonment that year. In a letter from Malcolm MacLeod on 29th October, John is informed of the motion to terminate his employment which was followed by a letter the following month informing him of the decision to dismiss. It is hard not to see State interference in this decision and

MacLean's papers show that he applied for re-instatement in 1919 and again before he died in 1923 and he was given a tale about the male lists not yet being made up. (12) This proves his need for economic security as well as his love of his vocation.

He continued this vocation in the field of adult education. He had started this in 1907. It wasn't French or Maths or life coaching that he taught. It had to be Karl. Marxian economics to be precise and it was a labour of love: to educate working class adults to understand the system that exploits them and to talk about the process of their liberation. His first classes were in Gourock, Falkirk and Pollokshaws. The glamour! And he was making a name for himself. Many socialists and trade unionists came to his classes even if they were not of a Marxist persuasion because they got the 'know how' about capitalism and because he was good. James Maxton, the future Labour MP, was one such pupil as were some of his later comrades such as Harry McShane and James McDougall.

It is useful to point out that he was not the first pioneer of adult, working class education. Willie Nairn from Brechin who moved to Glasgow was organising outdoor lectures on Capital. He was a stonebreaker and intellectual who was called, "a doughty champion of the teachings of Das Kapital." (13) This accolade could easily have applied to John MacLean. What made Nairn more of a pioneer was that he faced opposition as to the point of teaching Capital in a way that MacLean did not face.

Nairn is reported to have heckled William Morris, founder of the Socialist League, on economics and shouted a question from the floor asking if Morris accepted Marx's theory of value:

"I do not know what Marx's theory of value is and I'm damned if I want to know! Truth to say my friends I have tried to understand Marx's theory but political economy is not my line and much of it appears to be dreary rubbish."

Treacherous stuff to the committed Marxian. Morris reminded the audience of his own socialist credentials:

"It is enough political economy for me to know that the idle class is rich because they rob the poor. I see it with my eyes. I need to read no books to convince me of it." (14)

Morris had a point! It reminds me a bit like Billy Connolly's view of weather reading – just look out the window if you want to know the weather! Just go to any slum and you'll see poverty without ploughing through *Capital*. MacLean would have been as horrified as Nairn.

For MacLean, as with most people, there were different sides to his persona. He was the dour political activist, a non-smoker and did not partake of alcohol but he swore and had a sense of humour. He was also known to skip BSP committee meetings to go to Hampden Park to see Queens Park play. (15) Bunking off the political meetings to go to the football – my hero!

In 1911 the SDP became the British Socialist Party in line with many other organisations in Europe with an affiliation into the Labour Party. MacLean supported this move and was elected onto the Scottish District Committee. His star was on the rise. He argued for a Scottish national council within the new party to replace the district committee on the grounds that we were a nation not a district. He believed that ILP members would see sense and join the new party as a unified, socialist party: He issued a call to arms in Justice

"Meantime I appeal to all old comrades to be up and doing. Those of you who have lapsed, return: those of you who have lost heart, cheer up: those who have heart, pull in the indifferent and stimulate dormant or defunct branches. Let us 'ring in the new' with rejuvenated animation." (16)

It was non-stop political activity while he continued to forge a living by taking his evening classes and his speaking tours across Scotland and England. Nan mentions his Eastwood class which got a government subsidy:

"This was probably the only case in Britain in which Government funds were used to teach what were, in effect, subversive doctrines, Capital being the main textbook." (17)

When War broke out the classes helped to give the Clyde its Red reputation. Over 400 were enrolled onto his evening class in Bath Street in Glasgow's city centre which is really quite incredible. By 1917 the classes were on Sunday afternoons too and had over 500 enrolled in Glasgow with 125 in Greenock. He also visited London and classes sprang up there. He had drawing power and he was not working in isolation. Like minds and fellow teachers were involved in the setting up of a college with a curriculum - the Scottish Labour College. The ethos of the College was summed up on MacLean's membership card: "Knowledge must precede all intelligent action." His card had him on the Falkirk Economic and Industrial History class but he was all over. (18) The College was not one single building but spread out over various locations in Lanarkshire, Renfrewshire and Clydeside as well as in the big smoke itself.

The College had its own inexorable logic. Politicised workers were attending classes all over the west of the country. A college would formalise this. A college would coordinate this much better. A college could draw on the best educational techniques from other such colleges in England and beyond. It could expand as the word spread. Put simply: disparate, politicised workers could and should become a unified, politicised working class. These were heady aims and MacLean, MacDougall and the others behind this venture were absolutely justified in this belief.

It is maybe difficult for those of us, as I write, who use the internet and mobile phones and tablets to comprehend. Education is at our fingertips if we want it. During the upheaval of the First World War there were many looking for answers; for an alternative to the carnage that was taking place. The numbers who went to the classes cannot be underestimated. If the War was about big Empires fighting over booty then how could this be stopped? What could economics tell them – Marxian economics at that?

I have often wondered what one of MacLean's classes would be like. I have worked in training and think I am well versed in the subject. Everybody is an expert on training aren't they? Was this training? No, it was education. If I was a pupil, I would have stepped into one of his classes for the first time as a Socialist or a trade unionist with left sympathies. I would have looked at the classroom. Obviously, there would not have been flip charts or fancy projectors. Nope! There would have been tables and chairs and a chalkboard with formula on the board. A bit like The Prime of Miss Jean Brodie but for gruff working class Glaswegians.

And just like Miss Brodie, Mister MacLean would have had presence. He would have commanded the room. He had his own objectives but most importantly of all he had a vision. He wanted to teach Marxian economics to the Scottish working class. Indeed, he believed that this was his greatest crime in the eyes of the British Government. Annie Gordon attended his classes and called him a "marvellous teacher" with "no slant". He just gave the facts and spoke to you, "like a friend."
(19)

I'm a bit nosey so I would have 'people watched'. How attentive are the group? Are they taking notes? How many questions? Like all good teachers, MacLean would have instilled this fantastic ability to ask questions – the right questions, powerful questions – in his group.

He had answers too: scribbling on his chalk board the theories, enunciating the arguments in a coherent, passionate way. A lecture with passion that gripped us all. This was why war was raging all over Europe and Asia. This was why local capitalists and landlords were using the war to extract even more from working class people. Yet it may have felt new. Like most socialists I had probably read *The Ragged Trousered Philanthropist* by Robert Tressell and devoured *Justice* or *The Call* or *Forward* every week. I would have been familiar with Marx and Engels but probably hadn't read overly much of their works. Thanks to John MacLean I wouldn't need to read Capital because his lectures would bring it to life for me – in words, formula, gesticulations and energy.

MacLean had 16 lectures which he formulated for the Scottish Labour College. (20) This broke Marx down into bite size chunks but all the theory was there – the definitions and the equations and the world view of history. By lecture 8 we delegates would have been learning about the history of gold and its importance to capitalism. It really was taking *Capital* as his *Bible*. The premise was summed up in his opening Note:

"Political Economy or Economics is the science that examines the facts of the capitalist production and distribution of wealth to find out the underlying principles or laws." (21)

This was both the strength and the weakness of the College. As a science capitalism could be understood in its laws and functions. As an opposition, the working class would be made aware of its tasks and functions. The brains behind the operation were MacLean and MacDougall and they were certainly not limited in scope. They wanted to train technicians for the struggle. People who could bring about the revolution. They broadened the scope to the Cooperative movement which John knew well. They wanted history taught from a Marxian point of view and they also considered the technical skills such as English, algebra and maths.

(22) There is no doubt that this ethos was attractive to socialists across the Left political spectrum and many members of the non- Marxian Independent Labour Party would have benefitted from old Karl's analysis without drawing his conclusions. As MacLean and MacDougall put it:

"..a slight consideration of the vast problems and difficulties that the resumption of peace will raise for solution ought to show the need for a rapidly growing number of men able to defend the rights of the workers and enable them to proceed towards the full control of industry in a thoroughly disciplined fashion." (23)

This 'number of men' - not women - may have easily seen this defence of workers' rights as a Labour government. Yet it is certainly the case that MacLean as the socialist dominie played his part in this education.

The problem lay in the fact the College gave no consideration to culture and cultural questions. The College might as well have been based on the Moon for all its awareness of time and place in Scotland in 1916. The left nationalists of the Scottish Review criticised the College as a missed opportunity to raise questions of Scottish history and culture in the curriculum. The truth is that as loyal British socialists they just didn't know. As we shall see the Forward always had articles on Scottish history but from a north British perspective which didn't really get under the Scottish national question. The aim was to negate it not to promote it. MacLean himself had written under the pseudonym 'Gael' for the Justice newspaper for 3 and a half years and Gael was grappling not very successfully with its cultural significance. That would develop. The loyal Social Democrat took the same line as the cultural Scottish left wingers in Forward. Home Rule for Scotland but not independence or anything that would break up the working class movement. A Scottish Parliament could be used as an agitational tool but it was "sheer bluff" to see it as the solution to Scotland's social problems.

Likewise it was the "freaks of the propertied class" who were promoting the 600th celebration of the battle of Bannockburn which was, "fought by serfs for the benefit of a few barons." (24) A simplification you may think of the culmination of a 100-year war for Scottish independence. It was an analysis that was the product of the Scottish Left subsumed within a British Left and they were Jekyll and Hyde on cultural questions.

A further example, in Lecture 1 of his Notes MacLean gave the standard Marxian view of the stages of history from primitive communism through slavery and feudalism to present day capitalism. Did they really know what this primitive communism was? It was only in their later years that Marx and Engels studied anthropology and the cultural and political interactions of tribal societies. This questioned their own previously held view of progress; namely that it was historically progressive to sweep tribal societies away. The SLC curriculum lacked this cultural depth. They could have looked at Clan society and gained an understanding of where Culloden and the Clearances (Na Fuadaichean) would sit with the theory of capitalist development in Scotland but in the Scottish Labour College there was not a peep about such questions (25)

Perhaps Jim Young summed it up:

"Furthermore, university students of economics seldom acquired a broad culture any more than they do today." (26)

The most significant failing of the Scottish Labour College was still a cultural omission and still exists on the Left. Namely, what is socialism? It goes back to Marx himself. He critiqued capitalism but did not articulate in any great detail what it was being replaced with. This was not necessarily a bad thing. The Left was not and has never been one homogeneous mass. There was a fantastic opportunity to debate what socialism would look like.

A Labour College for Scotland.

For some years an Economic and Industrial History Class has been conducted in Glasgow during winter. This year the membership has reached almost 450. Out of the Class has been formed a Committee to promote a Labour College for Scotland. It is intended to call a Conference of delegates from all working class organisations early in 1916 to discuss the question and establish a more representative provisional committee for the realisation of a Labour College.

The Universities and other institutions for higher education have for their object the training of men and women to run capitalist society in the interests of the wealthy. We think the time has come for an independent College, financed and controlled by the working class, in which workers might be trained for the battle against the masters.

Such a College could be conveniently established in Glasgow.

Students might attend the College each day for three months.

The College might be run for three terms a year:—October till December, January till March, and April till June.

Such subjects as Economics; General and Industrial History; History, Structure, and Problems of Trade Unions; History, etc., of Co-operation; Laws affecting Labour; Business Methods applied to Labour Organisations; English Composition and Literature; Arithmetic and Algebra, etc., might be studied.

The only sound method of financing the scheme would be by the raising of a compulsory levy of a penny a month (say) through the trades organisations. A hundred pounds would thus be obtained from 2,000 workers in a year.

Students brought from the workshop might require maintenance bursaries rising to as much as £2 a week (say). A student per term at £2 a week, or three students a year, would cost £78 at the extreme rate. Out of the £100 would thus be left at least £22 for staffing and other expenses. The less the bursary the more students could avail themselves of the College privileges.

A hundred thousand workers at a farthing a week levy could in this way maintain a College of 50 Students a term, or 150 a year.

This need not prevent organisations other than trade unions, or individuals interested in education, giving grants for the support of the institution.

Students sent by contributing bodies would have to be selected by these bodies; by ballot and from one work or district per man preferably, so that each work or district would have its just number of students. Students ought to be selected for both enthusiasm for knowledge and activity in the workers' movement.

This need not preclude private students from attending the College on payment of a fixed fee.

The lecturers would be at the disposal of those willing to form evening and week-end classes, so that all might have a chance of benefiting by their support of the College.

The Board of Directors might be composed of representatives of contributing bodies, one per £100 or part thereof (say). The Directors ought to be selected in the same way as the students, the same qualifications being expected.

Remember that the Ruskin College at Oxford has been maintained by several trade unions and co-operative organisations, and that the Plebs College in London is maintained by the Welsh miners and the railwaymen.

It is surely now time for Scotland to shoot ahead and again assume that pride of place in education so long the boast of our fathers.

We know that you are interested in education. We therefore desire you to discuss this College proposition in your workshop, at your union branch, with your friends in the train, in Church, and in Chapel. If this is honestly done we feel confident that the College will be in full swing by October, 1916.

AGITATE! EDUCATE! ORGANISE!

Sub-Committee—

H. MULHOLLAND, Sheet Iron Workers.
JAS. NEILSON, Sheet Metal Workers.
W. LEONARD, Furnishing Trades.
JAS. D. MACDOUGALL, Lecturer in Industrial History.

D. ANDERSON, I.L.P.
P. M'DONALD, Postal Clerks.
G. SCOTT, N.U.C.

T. SCOTT, Kinning Park Co-op.
R. A. BRIDGES, A.S.E.
GEO. CUTHBERTSON, B.S.P.
JOHN MACLEAN, Lecturer in Economics.

Original leaflet drafted by MacLean and MacDougall with signatories.

44

It seems to me that the Marxists of the time seemed intent on organising mass working class parties which focussed on demands that would advance the interests of the working class but the goal became fuzzy. Britain was no different. The debates and discussions must have taken place but the concept of the great Social Democracy withered away and seemed to lose meaning.

Within the curriculum of the College an opportunity was lost to educate on the cultural side of the Social Democracy and how the various strands of the Left could work together for the common goal. In MacLean's writings in general he grapples with the subject at a very high level and again this is probably fair. No philosopher from on high should define socialism. Any debates that have taken place have not brought unity of purpose around a common ideal. Instead the debate was about winning the argument and uniting around the Party.

Bill Johnston, a founding member of the John MacLean Society and a former Lord Provost of Clydebank, used to tell the story of when he was a young member of the Communist Party an old comrade would say that when the Revolution comes everyone would have strawberries and cream in plenty. The young member would ask: "what if I don't like strawberries and cream?" "You'll have strawberries and cream whether you like it or no'", came the reply.

MacLean as the inspirational dominie would have been perfectly placed to discuss the various permutations of how socialists would like their strawberries but, like the Scottish national question, it just didn't seem to register. He was a classical Marxist and his job was to educate workers in the iniquities of the system and socialism would be, by default, democratic. Wouldn't it? He was the nineteenth century critic rather than the twentieth century ideologue.

A Glasgow Bulletin picture of an anti-War meeting. James Maxton is speaking with Guy Aldred, Harry Hopkins with MacLean on the bill too. "Note John MacLean's attitude" says the reporter at the bottom of the picture. MacLean and Maxton were fairly close. Below is a rare photo of them in conversation post war if the car is an indicator. (Courtesy - SRSM Website.)

It would be May 1920 before MacLean considered aspects of how his society of the future would look. He wrote an article for the Vanguard on *Banking in Bolshevist Britain*. By this time, he would have been secretly expelled from the British Socialist Party and have formed his Tramp Trust Unlimited of 5 activists. His newly resurrected newspaper, The Vanguard, would acquire a dissidence all of its own. In this article he was considering how a socialist state would regulate finance and the banks. He was articulating some thoughts on nationalisation and how this would apply internationally. The lack of depth showed in some of his naivety. For example, he believed that a fall in prices would force capitalists to hand over their businesses to a Labour government but he was starting to think about the, "facilitation of social ownership." (27)

It is striking that although these are just thoughts as to what the new society would be like, the dominie is still trying to create that capacity for thought and self-education:

"Do not worry as to whether the steps here indicated are the ones that will be taken or are worthy of adoption…This ought to incite readers to study Marxian literature, the mighty driving literature of today, the core of creative evolution in the reconstruction of society on a scientific basis."

He added a reminder to the Liberal Chancellor, Winston Churchill:

"Mr Churchill remember that, if you are unfit to rule, we of the working class are not only fit to rule, but we have the genius to scrap the organs of capitalism and create new and more scientific ones in their place."

And he finished with a little ditty:

"Churchill, Churchill now is the day

When Labour shall beat you in mental display." (28)

It was a positive affirmation of all he believed that
working class education could achieve. His messianic
zeal for the cause led him to believe the day was
coming. In 1920 there was a fresh intake into the
Scottish Labour College and MacLean was still a tutor.
His great strength and achievement was as a working
class educator who strived to create that genius to
scrap capitalism. It was not the fault of John MacLean
that we did not have the genius to implement the
socialist alternative.

His daughter, Nan, famously made a contribution from the
floor of a John MacLean event in Glasgow where she
scolded the Glasgow Labour City Council for wanting to
build a statue of him. The best monument, she said,
would be to build a proper Scottish Labour College. We
are still waiting. Then again, MacLean didn't see the
first one open its doors either. He was in jail for
being in the socialist army. James MacDougall read the
inaugural address to the College on his behalf while
MacLean was coming to prominence as an anti-War martyr
on the Clyde.

NOTES

1) Matt McGinn, *The Ballad of John MacLean*, in Thurso Berwick and TS Law, *Homage to John MacLean*, 1973 p x

2) John MacLean, Inaugural address to the Scottish Labour College...

3) The Gospel of John, 20:16.

4) *Attitude of the BSP*, Forward, 26/9/1914

5) Sylvia Pankhurst, *The Home Front,* 1932, p.265

6) Terry Brotherstone, Centenary Tribute - One Hundred Years of John MacLean (1879 - 1923) Labour Review, Vol 3, No. 4, p.217

7) Gael, Justice, 25/11/1911. The Moderator referred to was Dr. Wells.

8) Gael, Ibid, 7/6/1913.

9) Gael, Ibid., 28/5/1914

10)   John MacLean, *Education in Scotland*, Justice, 23/5/1918, in Jonson (ed), *Essential Writings and Speeches*, p. 28

11)   John MacLean Papers, NLS, Acc 4251

12)   John MacLean Papers, ibid.

13)   Hugh Savage and Les Forster, All for the Cause - Willie Nairn 1856 - 1902: Stonebreaker, Philosopher, Marxist, nd, p.29. The quote is from an SDF comrade, Hunter Watts.

14)   Savage and Forster, ibid, p. 30.

15)   Tom Bell, *John MacLean: Fighter for Freedom*, 1944, p.19

16)   John MacLean, *In the Rapids of Revolution*, 1978, p.69.

17)   Nan Milton, *John MacLean*, 1973, p. 41

18)   MacLean Papers, ibid.

19)   As told to Michael Donnelly in 1967 in Savage and Forster, ibid. p. 60

20)   *Notes of Lectures on Economics given by John MacLean*, published by the John MacLean Society, 1983.

21)   *Lectures*, ibid. Lecture 1, p.24

22)   *A Plea for a Labour College for Scotland,* co-
        written with James MacDougall in February 1916, In
        the Rapids of Revolution, p.   122
23)   Ibid. p.117.
24)   Gael, Justice, 5/3/1914 and 25/6/1914
25)   MacLean would later print an article from
        Ruaraidh Erskine of Mar on *Celtic Tribal Communism*
        in his Vanguard newspaper and also in his
        Supplement in the Socialist, December 1922.
26)   James D Young, James Connolly, James Larkin
        and John MacLean: the Easter Rising and Clydeside
        Socialism, in R Duncan and A McIvor, *Militant
        Workers: Labour and Class Conflict on the Clyde
        1900-50, Essays in honour of Harry McShane*, 1992,
        p. 169.
27)   John MacLean, *Banking in Bolshevist Britain*,
        The Vanguard, May 1920 (in Lectures, p. 56.
28)   MacLean, ibid, p. 57

Chapter 3 - Fame of sorts

We assure our comrades that we in Glasgow are internationalists first, last and all the time.

- John MacLean (1)

Socialism as a movement, as an effective countervailing tendency to the basic trend of the bourgeois world, went bankrupt in 1914…. I can say that at a stroke, national consciousness won ascendancy over socialist proletarian consciousness. A God took revenge whose existence had been denied.

- Mihaly Vajda (2)

Sir Edward Grey famously declared War on Germany on the floor of the House of Commons in August 1914 in defence of the small nation that was Belgium and, by implication, for all small nations. Apparently. Everybody knew that the war machines had been building in readiness and facing off to each other for years. Britain had a big empire and Germany wanted a big empire and the cousins in the various royal households kept quiet and supported their national governments as good monarchs should do despite their family connections. The English royal household had the good grace to change their surname from Saxe-Coburg-Gotha to Windsor and the name stuck.

The declaration of war caused understandable consternation among the wider populace as well as the jingoistic reactions and flag waving that was fuelled by the media against, "the Hun." A little less understandably this consternation was felt by the Left across Europe albeit for differing reasons.

Surely it was cut and dried. This was an imperialist war and the European Left were united in their hatred of imperialism. Socialists were nurtured in the belief that the workers had common cause across national borders.

The organisation of the socialist movement reflected this: the International with its own great anthem proclaiming, "The Internationale unites the human race." Many on the Left make assumptions regarding the nomenclature of the various Internationals. For clarity I will list them below.

The First International was the International Working Men's Association founded by Marx in the 1860's. This is not to be confused with the modern day working man's club although maybe Charlie and Freddie enjoyed a game of darts down at the local boozer in London on a Tuesday night. Who knows? Female readers will not need me to remind them of the significance in the name. The organisation was genuinely international but relatively small. If you want to dig deeper you may find the beginnings of the Left's wonderful capacity for fighting amongst themselves as the anarchist, Mikhail Bakunin, fell out with Marx and left the organisation.

The Second International was the Socialist International. This was Marxian inspired and was much larger consisting of the great socialist parties of Europe - mainly the German Social Democrats and the French Socialist Party. This was the great International organisation of the Social Democracy although highly Euro-centric. Interestingly, although the British Social Democratic Federation affiliated there was independent, Scottish representation at its founding conference in 1889 as Keir Hardie's Scottish Labour Party affiliated. The organisation became gradualist, more reform orientated and less revolutionary in approach and was to fall apart in August 1914.

The Third International followed the Bolshevik revolution in Russia and was the Communist International or Comintern for short. Its aim was to galvanise post-war revolutionary feeling and the revolutionary parties but as events transpired it came under the influence of Moscow as the revolutions across Europe were defeated and Russia was left in isolation. The Bolsheviks called the shots with the new Communist Parties as they were formed. There was also a Fourth International which had no other name and composed of the dissidents to the new Communist Parties. This was formed in the late 1920's after MacLean's death. However, the Scottish Workers Republican Party, which he formed, joined this International as did some of his old comrades – Sylvia Pankhurst and Jim Larkin., In keeping with the old maxim that things go full circle, the Fourth iteration was as small as the first but without the darts and the dominoes. There hasn't been a fifth one to my knowledge.

I mention this because internationalism was the watchword. The Internationale was and is the anthem. The Collins English dictionary defines internationalism as:

"The ideal or practice of cooperation or understanding for the good of all nations." (3)

The Left defined it as working class solidarity and common cause. They didn't pay much attention to the composition of the word. Inter-nationalism. They didn't try to understand the various components that make up the identity of working class people. Being working class defined their exploitation and their poverty and their status. Gender, religion, nationality and race defined their personal identity. It is a crucial difference.

Marx grappled with contemporary issues in his time – slavery in America; the Irish and Polish struggles for national independence; the 'Woman Question' but he provided no definitive answers that would satisfy the protagonists of these struggles. The Marxist line evolved into the belief that organised labour in its struggle to emancipate itself would by definition emancipate all oppressed groupings. A view emerged that by struggling independently feminists, Polish nationalists, anti-slavery groups were distracting from the class struggle.

It seemed simple then that in 1914 the International would stand firm and class interests would win the day.

As mentioned the Second International comprised of large socialist parties who had participated in electoral politics in their respective countries. When the national parliaments of Europe discussed supporting their national governments war effort then the "god took revenge whose existence had been denied." The main parties of the Left in Germany and France and Italy voted with their national governments to give "war credits." In Britain the Labour Party leader, Keir Hardie, adopted a pacifist line but did not stop members of his Party from joining a war coalition. The International disintegrated. The scale of the disintegration was summed up by Tom Anderson:

"Labour leaders fell over the top of one another to become recruiting sergeants."

He then went on to quote Lossiemouth's own Ramsay MacDonald, future Labour leader and ex Secretary of the Scottish Home Rule Association, writing in September 1914:

"I want the serious men of the Trade Unions, the brotherhoods, and similar movements to face their duty. **England has need of you.**" Anderson's emphasis (4)

This was a familiar tale across the British Left. The BSP leadership of Hyndman and Belfort Bax also supported the British side. MacLean was not just opposing the War but he was also in opposition to his own Party leadership and his initial anti-War effort reflected this. Not only was he organising meetings in Glasgow's Bath Street to protest against the slaughter and its causes but he was also using the columns of Justice to raise what he felt was a "class patriotism":

"The absurdity of the present situation is surely apparent when we see British socialists going out to murder German socialists with the object of crushing Kaiserism and Prussian militarism." (5)

Surely this was the business of German Social Democrats and the BSP should be taking on their capitalist enemy at home. MacLean never wavered from this line during the entirety of the War and it led him to prison three times.

It would not be long before Gael stopped contributing to Justice. The Glasgow District Committee decided to publish their own newspaper, The Vanguard. MacLean was instrumental in getting the Glasgow Aggregate meeting to adopt the following resolution on 3rd January 1915:

"That this meeting of Glasgow members of the BSP, recognising that this War has been brought about by the intrigues of the capitalist and landlord interests of all the countries involved; and the workers of the world will obtain no advantages out of the war, determines to do all it can to peacefully stop the war at the earliest moment." (6)

Hyndman and *Justice* continued to take a jingoist, pro-British line. It is important to remember that opposition to the war, as with conscientious objection, was a highly courageous stand to take. If your son was away fighting on the Western Front and the media heralded their bravery and the righteousness of the cause that they were fighting for (namely, King and Country and poor little Belgium) then the anti-war socialists were confronting emotion. During the course of the war, Scotland alone lost 110,000 men. As Murray Pittock put it:

"Scotland, with a tenth of the population, contributed over 20 per cent of Britain's war dead and 26 per cent of enlisted Scots died." (7)

This statistic gave many working class Scottish families an interest in the war effort. The courage of the pacifists and the resonance of this statistic would only become apparent as the carnage became apparent. MacLean was the top and hem of this story. He became the figurehead of anti-war resistance on Clydeside and the scale of his task would have become crystal clear to him when he gave a lecture to his, old Cooperative comrades in Renfrewshire in December 1914. His talk was summed up by its title - The War: its cause and cure. His audience would have expected his Marxian analysis of the rush for empires, militarism and that this would continue while capitalists ran the world. The solution I will quote in full because in its answer it gives us a thread to the Marxist republican who would emerge, after some soul searching and education, from the other side of the war:

"When industries were thus in the hands of the workers, rent and other forms of plunder would cease and capitalism would meet a well-merited death: national co-operation would logically develop and national independence would force the respective states to justly exchange their surplus produce.; and this would call into existence a world parliament binding race to race and man to man in one universal brotherhood. In such a commonwealth it would become transparently clear that the making of the munitions of war or the maintenance of a soldier class was sheer, absurd and barbarous economic waste. Consequently, armies and navies must vanish and war, the fiend, disappear…" (8)

You might think that he was a dreamer but he wasn't the only one as John Lennon would have said 60 years later! MacLean understood internationalism. He didn't just practice it, he got it. This consistent line led him to really understand British imperialism too which is why his later election manifestoes, after he had broken with British socialism, take exactly the same line. It didn't, however, go down too well with the Co-operative Movement who also adopted a pro-war line and he wasn't asked back.

The message was disseminated through the *Vanguard* and *Forward*. The activism was at the workplace. The strength

of the trade union movement on Clydeside had mobilised
against the dilution of labour and the manoeuvres of the
employers in using the opportunity of the war to
profiteer still further. A deputation of Glaswegian
bosses approached the Government asking for a martial
law that they could administer locally. (9) In for a
penny, in for a pound! The unions organised into the
Clyde Labour Witholding Committee in February 1915 and,
"pressed the claim that the war in France should take
second place to the class struggle at home." (10) This
would become the Clyde Workers Committee (CWC) later
that year.

MacLean was there during all the key battles and, to be
fair, the key players of Red Clydeside cut their teeth
in these struggles. Willie Gallacher did some fantastic
work organising the rank and file to act in the
interests of the working class where the union
leadership and Labour Party were collaborating with the
Government. An estimated 10,000 workers were out on
unofficial strike after Weir's engineering firm in
Cathcart, on the south side of Glasgow, brought in
American engineers on higher wages.

Characteristically, MacLean was on the outside looking
in with a puritanical stance. He was never actually on
the CWC. For John, the struggle was political, not
merely industrial, Again, with an eye on things to come
MacLean chastised Gallacher after a speech in Bath
Street where he never even mentioned the War. (11) This
was not acceptable to MacLean who felt that the link had
to be made between the anti-war struggle and the rank
and file stand against the Government. This didn't
necessarily go down too well within sections of the
left. Helen Crawford of the Women Workers Guild and a
prominent activist on the Clyde recalled John spending
his whole speech outside Weir's Munitions factory in
Cathcart attacking the CWC. And she did not see this as
justified pointing out that Gallacher had criticised
proposed conscription too! (12)

The vociferous nature of MacLean's stand brought him to the attention of the increasingly paranoid Government who had passed the Defence of the Realm Act. It was his lectures and the alleged language that brought him to trial. The sword of Damocles must have been hanging over him because the Catholic Socialist Notes column in the Forward (John Wheatley), a month before his trial, wrote:

"Mr. John McLean (sic), if still at liberty, will be our lecturer on Sunday. John's ability and fearless ness have singled him out as one of the great rebel leaders of our time, and consequently, one of the first subjects of persecution. Our rulers fear McLean more than they do the whole Labour Party." (13)

In November he was arrested on two linguistic charges: firstly, that he said, in effect, God damn the Army; secondly, that he called soldiers murderers. It was exaggerated in order to get their man. John refuted the prosecution evidence with characteristic eloquence and stated boldly and powerfully:

"I have been enlisted for 15 years in the socialist army. It is the only army worth fighting for; God damn all other armies." (14)

This is what he had actually said in a speech and he repeated it to the court. He did not say that the soldiers were murderers but those who sent them to war were! (15) The socialist army was the only army he could have recognised. It had killed nobody, invaded nowhere and sought to raise the red flag of liberation, peacefully, all over the planet. His actions and words were consistent in those 15 years since he had discovered Marx. He got a £5 fine or 5 days in prison and he was never going to pay the fine.

His 5 days at His Majesty's Pleasure had been as a result of his revolutionary activity. He was one of many men of the Left who stood by the mostly female rent strikers of Glasgow who themselves were standing up to

unscrupulous and rack-renting landlords. The
contemporary photograph showed the irony of these
patriotic landlords evicting women and their families
(while the men-folk were away fighting on the western
front for the King) and the children waved their little
Union Jacks. Councillor Paddy Dollan of the ILP wrote
that the rent strikers won 3 major concessions: i) the
Factors had to declare publicly that they would not
raise the rents of the families of dependents of
soldiers and sailors; ii) the Government were compelled
to set up a committee of inquiry to look at the causes
of the rent increases and iii) the struggle prevented
the eviction of rent strikers. (16) The socialist army
mobilised and won a victory. MacLean's part in the
struggle was recognised in January 1916 when he was
elected secretary of the Scottish National Labour
Housing Association which was set up to prevent further
rack renting across the country.

MacLean's activities were also dangerous because he was
uniting the Clyde with the wider European movement
against the war. In October 1915 a Russian emigrè called
Peter Petroff came back to Glasgow. He was a member of
the BSP and in fact had stood for the national
executive. He had been in Glasgow for a spell after he
left his homeland in 1905 after a failed revolution.
Petroff played a pivotal educational role:

"It was through Petroff's lectures and talks that
Glasgow socialists heard for the first time of the
political debates within Russian Social Democracy and of
the importance of such figures as Lenin and Trotsky."
(17)

Petroff and his German wife, Irma stayed with the
MacLeans in Auldhouse Road. MacLean and Petroff seemed
to be a political match made in heaven. As Smyth and
Rodgers put it, MacLean 'advocated revolution' whereas
Petroff had 'encountered it.' (18) This made them the
ones with the revolutionary analysis. Peter was in
contact with those on the continent and it was probably

from his emigrè friend that MacLean learned about the
International Socialist conference in Zimmerwald in
Switzerland. No BSP delegates were given a visa to
attend but Petroff was in the know. MacLean could share
some knowledge in the Vanguard about how the European
Left were lining up and he spared no criticism for his
own Party's leadership:

"Faithful social democrats here have been led a sorry
dance by the bourgeois members of the central branch of
the BSP. Our business is to trust ourselves and our
cause and line up with our world comrades as quickly as
we can." (19)

Willie Gallacher

MacLean was thus a dangerous revolutionary to both the
British State and the leadership of the British
Socialist Party. He didn't have any epiphany moment

during his 5 days in jail so he came out to more of the same. And it was ferocious! He lost his job as a teacher, as we have seen, in November. The BSP leadership stepped up the pressure against Petroff in an editorial in Justice in December 1915 entitled *Who and What is Peter Petroff?* The intention was to paint him as a shadowy, spy-like figure. Characteristically, John MacLean jumped to his comrade's defence. Petroff was playing a key part in the Clyde's revolt and he was influential in letting the activists in the CWC and the local Party know what was going on in Europe but significantly, "Petroff does not do our thinking." (20)

The central leadership were under pressure from rank and file activists across the Party. Maybe they were using Petroff to deflect from their own troubles. The Government were pushing ahead in early 1916 with conscription to boost the amount of all too human fodder for cannons at the front. It was a sign of how desperate the position was as stalemate enveloped the fighting at the Front. MacLean and Petroff threw themselves into this campaign which was highly seditious.

Peter was arrested first of all at a meeting in Fife in late December and detained and sent to an internment camp called The Institute in Islington where he was held until his repatriation to Russia in August 1917. MacLean was refused access to visit him. Soon he would have his own troubles to seek as he was arrested and taken, in Nan's words, as a prisoner of war to Edinburgh castle on 6th February and would be charged with sedition. This was part of a wider State crackdown on the Clyde activists as Gallacher, John Muir (of the CWC), Manny Shinwell (of the Labour Party) were also arrested. Show trials took place and the Red Clydesiders were deported to Edinburgh!

MacLean seemed quite upbeat as he answered his charges from the dock for the second time. His entourage had listened to the fiddle and tin whistle on the train through to the capital and all had sung the Red Flag. In the dock he referred, humorously, to a meeting at Nelson's Pillar in Glasgow Green against the passing of the Military Service bill. He was telling the loyalists in the crowd about German clocks:

"You men are all patriots and won't use any goods of German manufacture. I understand that you have all got German alarm clocks to waken you in the morning. As patriots you surely can't continue to use these. You should pawn them or sell them. Be sure to do it all at one time and then you will all sleep in in the morning." (21)

The judge, Lord Strathclyde, must have liked his German alarm clock. He told MacLean that his previous light sentence had failed and so the options were penal servitude or death. The crime for his sedition would be 3 years penal servitude. He served the first month in Calton jail in Edinburgh before being transferred to Peterhead.

The campaign to release him began immediately. Sales of work were held for his family in their distress. The ILP, the BSP and the Scottish Labour College all raised MacLean's case. One can only surmise how Agnes must have felt. She was political in her own right and would have seen the bigger picture. Or was it the bigger picture? What was bigger in her life than her unemployed husband being in jail up in the north east while you have the two weans to raise in his absence for a potential three years. Poor John didn't really get this if his first letter is anything to go by:

"On no account worry about me…I have no reason to feel depressed even if kept here for three years…Supposing I knew there wouldn't be a Socialist in Scotland when I came out I would not let that worry me but resolve to come out and begin the good work again." (22)

To be fair to George Barnes (his local MP), although MacLean did not believe him, he had been writing on his behalf at Agnes' instigation. Back in 1917, he wrote to

Munro enquiring as to his release from prison (on 14/2/17 to be precise.) He said that if the Secretary of State could remit the whole or part of the unexpired portion of the sentence then he would be "glad." This was provoked by a very poignant letter from Agnes to him. Nan had been seriously ill the last two months, "and I have felt just desperate to have my husband beside me." Her long night watches had made up her mind to do all she could for his release. This was backed up by a letter to Munro too. Agnes was digging deep again and it must have felt like a tired old 78-inch-long play record. (23)

Much has been made since MacLean's death of his mental state. This originated from his medical papers during this stint in prison. The Secretary of State felt that he was "evidently a highly strung, neurotic subject." No surprises there then! However, this view of MacLean as a mad man was later taken on by the nascent Communist Party. An overlooked aspect of his prison record comes across in a Medical record of 14/6/17 which put the delusions as those of grandeur:

"…he readily becomes excited; and it is reasonable to believe that if he were placed in the company of those who would encourage and applaud him – for he is greedy for admiration – his mental condition would suffer seriously." (24)

These were the words of JS Devon, the prison doctor who cited Perth's regime as calming him but the visits from friends triggered the above. Politicos would do well to ponder this view. Devon may have been way off the mark but his observations get me thinking of politics as a drug to the mind and the ego – especially in men. The speeches, the lectures, the big meetings were MacLean's life. There would have been angst at not having them there. It didn't make him mad or neurotic just flawed and human.

The attached report memorandum also deals with MacLean's view that his food and medicines were being tampered

with and there was nothing that Dr Devon could do to
convince him otherwise. John looked 10 years older due
to the fact that his hair had gone white and Devon
observed that he was markedly worse after visits from
his wife: Agnes' news made him more excited and
irritable. These are interesting insights into MacLean's
life and while they are certainly not fact (but the
observations of a prison doctor) they open the door to
what MacLean thought and felt in prison at a time of
great personal and family turmoil.

In an interesting note he mentioned that MacLean's
heroics were harmful to him.

Surmise, again, could maybe help with making sense of
the level of re-assurance that Agnes may have felt at
her husband's words. For hubby, it was all for the cause
- the dangerous narcotic. He served a year in jail
beginning on 13th April. He missed the tumultuous events
in Dublin two weeks later. He missed the BSP's spring
conference at the same time which also missed the
tumultuous events in Dublin as we shall see. This
conference did kick out Hyndman and his clique from the
Party and John MacLean was elected in absentia onto the
national executive of the Party. He was becoming famous,
of sorts, as the figurehead of the revolutionary
movement in Glasgow, Scotland, Britain and became a
household name as public enemy number one or as a
working class hero depending upon your viewpoint - even
in European circles.

The Forward from 14/7/17 acknowledged MacLean's release
with a front page article - *Back to the World Again!* He
does thank George Lansbury and the Russian workers for
securing his release; he does use the opportunity to
call for the release of Peter Petroff and his family.
Agnes gets a mention for keeping him on his toes in
terms of food expenditure and how this impacts on the
consulate.

When he did get back to his own household he was true to his word. It was back to the good work of the socialist army. The Russian wing was planning big things.

NOTES

1) John MacLean, *Zimmerwald*, Vanguard, October 1915, in *In The Rapids of Revolution*, 1978 p. 93

2) Mihaly Vajda. *The State and Socialism: Political Essays*, 1989, p.91

3) *Collins Concise Dictionary and Thesaurus*, 1998 edition p501

4) Comrade Tom, Comrade John MacLean, MA, 1938, p. 15-16

5) Letter in Justice, 17/9/1914, the Rapids, ibid., p. 76.

6) Quoted in Tom Bell, *John MacLean: A Fighter for Freedom*, 1944, p.30

7) Murray Pittock, A New History of Scotland, 2003, p.267

8) MacLean, In the Rapids, ibid. p. 79

9) Keith Middlemass, *Politics in Industrial Society*, 1980, p.72

10)   Middlemass, ibid. p. 73

11)   James Smyth and Murdoch Rodgers, *Peter Petroff and the Socialist Movement in Britain, 1907-18*, This essay appears in John Slatter (ed.) *From the Other Shore: Russian Political Emigrants in Britain, 1880-1917*, 1984, Note 36, p.114

12)   Helen Crawford in evidence to MacLean's trial for sedition in 1916. John MacLean papers, Mitchell Library, Glasgow, TD 260.

13)   Catholic Socialist Notes, Forward, 23/10/1915

14)   MacLean, Speech from the dock, 1915, In the Rapids, ibid. p. 93

15)   Report of the trial in Forward, 20/11/1915

16)   Councillor Paddy Dollan, Forward, 23/10/1915

17)   Smyth and Rodgers, ibid. p. 105

18)   Smyth and Rodgers, ibid. p. 112

19)   MacLean, Zimmerwald, The Vanguard, October 1915, In the Rapids, ibid, p.92-3

20)   MacLean, Letter to Justice, 30/12/1915 in In the Rapids, p. 94

21)   MacLean, Speech from the Dock, 1916, In the Rapids, ibid. p. 97

22)   Nan Milton, *John MacLean*, 1973, p.134
23)   Ibid, HH16/123.
24)   JS Devon, prison doctor, Ibid.

Chapter 4 – His Finest Hour (and a quarter)

"He advocated a Social Revolution by Bolshevist methods, and alas, the bulk of the workers do not want a Social Revolution by any method, but go on rivet hammering competitions and scrambling for overtime and regard the John Macleans as decent enough but a bit off."

- Tom Johnston (1)

"The bourgeois stands like a hungry dog

Wordless he stands like a question mark.

And the old world stands like a mongrel dog

Right behind him, its tail between its legs."

- Alexander Blok (2)

The Bolsheviks seized power in Russia in November 1917. Their programme was simple – "Peace, Bread, Freedom. All power to the Soviets!" They had replaced another revolutionary regime, namely that of Alexander Kerensky who had headed up a broadly reformist socialist coalition whose fatal mistake was to continue the War against Germany on the Allied side.

Tom Anderson said that when John heard the news that the Bolsheviks had seized power he just held Comrade Tom's hand tightly staring in delight. John had been freed on licence in June and went straight to work as a dominie in the Scottish Labour College. His time and reflections in Peterhead prison must have focused on education and his classes and the fruits of his theorising led to a pamphlet published by the college, *The war after the war in the light of working class economics*. This was one of MacLean's longer written works and gives a very powerful argument that the current war had logic and it would manifest itself again without social change and working class power. Capitalists and industrialists knew no different and would act no different.

He did not talk in terms of a national victory for anyone – Britain or Germany. He talked about the next phase of capitalism and how the capitalists of these countries were gearing up for the next phase of their industrial expansion. In reference to Britain specifically, and in Marxian language he gave them their own appeal:

"Capitalists of the empire, unite! You have nothing but an empire to lose, you have a world to win!" (3)

MacLean's strong subject knowledge comes out. He studied industrial methods and developments in Britain and internationally. He knew how this applied to working class communities and he referenced reports into poverty in communities in Glasgow and Edinburgh, York and London across the border. He could see the expansion of the United States economy across the American continent and into Asia (which informed some of his later writings on British – American rivalry.) It was MacLean the working class educator and propagandist at his best. He looked to the Bolsheviks who, "have given the world the lead." (4) You would expect no different from the foremost revolutionary in the British Isles. The workers were in power in a huge country that would have repercussions across Europe.

The strange thing is that there are no major writings on Russia in the short period after the Revolution. No big articles, no big letters just references. Nan Milton felt that it was a pity there were no records of his speeches post Revolution. (5) This was not technically true. Nan was not to know (or could not divulge due to the Official Secrets Act) that the police were keeping an excellent record of his speeches and lectures with details of venue and the title too! However, it is still very strange. He was very excited and there were certainly avenues to share this excitement in the *Call* or the ILP's *Forward*. The only explanation can be the lack of information. His old buddy, Peter Petroff, was still in the Institute and he was a key source of information.   That is conjecture. On his release though MacLean stepped up the calls for the release of Petroff and Irma. In quite a heartfelt letter to the Call MacLean set out exactly what Petroff was about - a fine internationalist with a head for tactics. He learned English in MacLean's house but MacLean learned much more:

"He and I fought over Britain's tactical moves eg, in Salonica. Petroff has proved to be right up till the present: MacLean wrong. I am not afraid to admit it." (6)

This was not something that the egotistic Clydesider admitted too often. His affection for his Russian friend was deep as he requested his comrades in the BSP campaign for the release of "a clean fighter for freedom and justice, an innocent man." This was not the view of the leadership of the Party.

It is certainly true that his pro Revolutionary excitement was also shared in less expected circles. Ruaraidh Erskine of Mar exclaimed, "Praise to the Bolsheviks! Honour to the Revolutionaries!" He held the Revolution up to his fellow Scottish nationalists because Russia was carrying the banner of "universal national rights." By calling for self-determination for all nations, no Annexations and an end to international enmity and greed Erskine believed that only the Bolsheviks proclaimed a "clean and lasting peace." (7)

It was also true that the Russians knew about MacLean. Along with Karl Liebknecht in Germany and Viktor Adler in Austria the boy from Pollokshaws was made an Honorary President of the first All Russian Congress of Soviets. On 30th January 1918 the Glasgow Herald announced that the Russian Government had sent a wireless announcing that John Reed was to be the Soviet Consul in New York. Reed had been the eye witness author of one of the first accounts of the revolution for a western audience, *Ten*

Days that Shook the World. The wireless also announced
that John Maclin (sic) was to be the Soviet Consul in
Glasgow. (8) It was an honour and very strong
recognition. It was recognition of his heroism in
resisting the War, in his commitment to the Zimmerwald
position, his education of the workers in the face of
pro war propaganda and his defence of the young Soviet
Republic.

Shortly after the Revolution Georgy Chicherin, the
Soviet Commissar for Foreign Affairs was interred.
MacLean passed on the regards of 'thousands' of Scottish
friends:

"I am running 9 Marxist classes every week with a
membership of about a thousand and the members are being
kept up to date on your affairs. MacDougall is running 6
classes and is doing likewise. Marxism is growing
rapidly and with it then interest in and importance of
all connected with Russia, yourself included although
you refuse to admit the correctness of Marxism." (9)

MacLean may soon indeed have been a consul but he was no
diplomat! Still Chicherin received some funds, the
Forward newspaper and some real encouragement.

The new Consul took to this honour and set up offices in
12 South Portland Street. His Secretary was the Russian
émigré, Louis Shammes. MacLean saw his role as a
supportive role for the dependents of those Russian
exiles who had been repatriated to fight for the Russian
Army. He used his position to officially criticise these
deportations and wrote that many exiled women came to
him with stories of, "depression, disease and death."
(10)

MacLean was well aware of the pro-revolutionary
sentiments within the exiled community. Lanarkshire, in
particular, had a strong Lithuanian community and their
exile was a political exile and the held ahostility to
the Tsarist regime. There were gun running activities
from Lanarkshire to the Baltic after the failed

Revolution in 1905 and John knew of the activities of the Lithuanian Peter the Painter from Craigneuk as well as the veteran socialist, George Turgeloovis who was in the same SDF branch as MacLean back in the day. (11)

It is also fair to say that if MacLean knew then the British State certainly knew. The recently opened criminal papers of MacLean confirm this. It is worth bearing in mind that MacLean had taken up this post as Consul while he was still on licence. "The case of John MacLean is one of considerable notoriety in the Clyde District." So wrote the Secretary of State for Scotland, Robert Munro on 20th February 1918 while also noting that with Louis Shammas (sic) as his Secretary, another "Russian alien, Urbanovich" from the base in 12 South Portland Street, they posed a "combination unquestionably dangerous to the peace of the Clyde." (12)

They were, predictably, being watched. It was felt that Shammes individually did not pose a threat but in combination with MacLean he caused much alarm to the authorities to the point that they felt that he had to be dealt with. Shammes addressed a crowd of 15000 at a pro-Russian rally on Glasgow Green in March. A police report concluded that with his association with MacLean, his influence on his Russian compatriots was "pernicious." His continuing presence "could not be tolerated." (13)

In a letter of 14th March, H Guest at HQ, Scottish Command, Edinburgh said that he was happy to hear that 'Shammas' was being repatriated. Internal memos and discussions continued. MacLean's position as "alleged Bolshevik Consul General for Scotland" made the position "delicate" according to Haldane, the General Officer, C in C, Eastern Command (12/3/18.) In the attached report MacLean seemed to be goading the police. MacLean had written to state that he would no longer be reporting in as it was meaningless in view of his position as Consul and "derogatory" to the great Russian Republic. (This was brought to the attention of Munro himself.)

The C in C of the Scottish Command, JS Ewart, felt that there were two options for MacLean - cancellation of his licence or prosecution. He favoured the latter so that there could be no claims of victimisation. The same memo called for the prosecution of James MacDougall and the deportation of Shammes. (14) While it is clear that the State did not want to accord MacLean any official recognition as Consul, they also realised that they had to tread carefully. He was in contact with Litvinov who was the official Ambassador in London.

So they played a long game. Police spies transcribed his speeches. If MacLean was a modern pop star they would have bought every CD! These were the speeches that Nan could not write about for example in a speech in the Co-operative Hall, Cambuslang on Problems of the Hour (10th February 1918) the police gained 'down tools' evidence and transcribed that the workers should take the food surplus. I liked MacLean's solution to end the war:

"The soldiers are sick of the war. I am quite prepared to send Lloyd George, the British Government and all the patriots who wish the war to continue, out to the front trenches and give them a week of it. My friends, you can take it from me that even that old fire-eater, Sir Edward Carson would wish the war to stop right away. (Laughter)" (15)

Another good example came from a City of Glasgow police report on a BSP meeting on 20th January addressed by MacLean on "The working class: its position and prospects" in Glasgow's Stockwell Street. John had called for "maximalist socialism or nothing" and had called himself a socialist democrat. In a recurring theme in the police file, they felt that he was mental! "Mentally unsound and verging on collapse," to use their words. At the end of the meeting MacLean called for three cheers for the Russian revolution, "which were heartily given. A youth at the back of the hall called for three cheers for the British Revolution but there was no general response." This was duly recorded by the police groupies without comment. Was revolution ok in Russia but not for the UK? Didn't John MacLean even raise a cheer?

In another speech in County Durham the former Calvinist trainee teacher stated that the mantle of Christ had descended and fallen on the Bolsheviks! (16) This was either a completely bizarre or entirely logical statement for a convert to make. MacLean as a lover of poetry may also have been aware of Blok's post revolution poem entitled, *The Twelve*. This controversial poem – brutal, iconoclastic, challenging and one of the real examples of the revolution unleashing cultural creativity and energy – imaged the Apostles and who had descended and fallen upon the Bolshevik Twelve?:

"And so they keep a martial pace.

Behind them follows the hungry dog.

Ahead of them – with bloody banner,

Unseen within the blizzard's swirl

Safe from any bullet's harm

With gentle step above the storm

In the scattered pearl like snow.

Crowned with a wreath of roses white

Ahead of them – goes Jesus Christ." (17)

John MacLean was either crazier or more switched on than you think.

With such heavy police spying it would not be long before MacLean was back in the dock – 9th May to be precise. By calling on the workers to down tools and take food it was the road to sedition. It was also a follow through on Ewart's preferred course of action.

"It has been said that they cannot fathom my motive. For the full period of my active life I have been a teacher of economics to the working classes and my contention has always been that capitalism is rotten to its foundations and must give place to a new society." (18)

So began his speech from the dock at trial number 3 in the High Court in Edinburgh. He conducted his own defence and used the next 75 minutes to point the finger at the system, to be the accuser and condemn this obscene war as he had done twice previously. This time his eloquence set the speech and MacLean himself apart.

It was a classic speech in the real sense of the term. It was a speech that was very aware of its historical backdrop coming to the end of a War that many were weary of. The orator was also very aware of his part in the struggle against this carnage and also used it as an opportunity to warn those who would listen that such wars were in the genetic make-up of capitalism. As such, it has become a famous and oft-quoted speech on the Left. He pointed the finger back at the system as the accuser not the accused of this murderous system whose blood was still dripping from head to toe. In the dock was the accuser of capitalism and it remains a striking revolutionary image at the tail end of the First World War. It truly was a fine enunciation of socialist internationalism by a seasoned veteran.

Yet it is all too easy to forget that 'MacLean the accuser' was for the press and the photo ops (nobody knows to this day how the photograph was taken in the court room.) This is superficial as a reading of the speech shows that it was the same old dominie who had a new audience for his lecture. In the guise of the Philadelphia lawyer conducting his own defence he let rip with a passionate critique of the capitalist system, War and the inhumanity of both. He could have been in Bath Street or in the Scottish Labour College. Instead, he was in the High Court in the capital city. The other lawyers and note takers, visitors and Lord Strathclyde himself were his audience. The only difference was in the gravitas of the occasion but it was the same old John MacLean and he wasn't shy.

John MacLean in the dock, 9th May 1918. No one knows how the photo was taken.

He did, of course, deal with his charges namely that he had urged the workers to "down tools" and that they should take food if they were hungry. One of his offending speeches used the Bible as his guide with the instruction: "Thou shalt not kill! Thou shalt not steal!" John knew the hypocrisy that he was exposing better than the hypocrites themselves. He knew the theology. Giving good news to the poor, setting captives free and feeding the hungry were all part of setting the downtrodden free weren't they? John knew that these fine words and prayers were a challenge to the actions of the established Christian churches and their Establishment adherents. He continued to call their bluff:

"I pointed out to the workers that what was necessary if they stopped work was the getting of food. There had been a shortage; the Government had held the supplies, for several reasons probably – perhaps to get this rationing passed, in order to have a tight hold on food and also lest the people get out of hand in reference to this Manpower Bill. I knew that there was plenty of food in stores in Glasgow." (19)

He really exposed the cynicism of a government using food as a pawn while there was a war raging and that was why he was facing Lord Strathclyde again in a court room in Edinburgh. The speech was also a chance to elaborate on the theme of his Labour College pamphlet on the *War after the War*. MacLean had an excellent grasp backed up by his reading, of international affairs, He understood what would now be called geo-politics be it from a British, American or Japanese perspective. He could cut a swathe through the jingoism and false patriotism just as strongly as he did in 1914. The socialists were right then and they were still right. His class patriotism meant that he was no traitor to his country merely loyal to his class and it was his class that the rulers feared not Germany.

"My own people are the workers here and the workers in Germany and elsewhere. It was not the workers who instigated the war. The workers have no economic interest to serve as a consequence of the war, and because of that, it is my appeal to my class that makes me a patriot so far as my class is concerned..."

MacLean did not go on to articulate who "his country" was. He did proclaim:

"...and when I stand true to my class, the working class, in which I was born, it is because my people were swept out of the Highlands, and it was only because of my own ability that I remained."

It was a powerful, powerful statement of personal identity that explained who and what he was about. A real, moral righteousness based on his own class morality thundered out.

"We are out for life and all that life can give us. I therefore took what action I did in the light of what was transpiring inside Russia, inside Austria, inside Germany." (20)

The Gaels have a beautiful word for life in this context - beatha (pronounced beh-ha.) He would have heard it a lot growing up in its Biblical context. As a middle aged socialist he knew that across Europe there were revolts to give life back to people and to end the carnage and the despair and the hunger. To propose the opposite was hypocrisy:

"In the plunge into the war we have the abolition of constitutional methods, and therefore I contended, and I contend today that if it is right and proper on the part of the Government to throw aside law and order-constitutional methods - and to adopt methods that mankind has never seen before then it is equally right that the members of the working class, if war is not going to cease in a reasonable time, should bring about a reasonable settlement, and a reasonable settlement to the workers is no victory to either side." (21)

He had paid tribute to Russia where the new regime was out for life and positive change for their people. He now went on to predict what would happen - further empire building between countries and between capitalist enterprises themselves. He had nothing to retract or to apologise for and in a rousing finale touching on morality but based on his vision of the future, John MacLean spoke:

"No matter what your accusations against me may be, no matter what reservations you keep at the back of your head, my appeal is to the working class. I appeal exclusively to them because they and they only can bring about the time when the whole world will be in one brotherhood on a sound economic foundation. That, and that alone, can be the means of bringing about a reorganisation of Society. That can only be obtained when the people of the world get the world and retain the world." (22)

MacLean would have sat down, tired after a 75-minute speech. Not surprisingly, Lord Strathclyde did not say, "Wow! I'd never thought about things like that before!" Instead the judge took a pop at MacLean by warning the jurors that he did not pretend to know what went on, "in the dark recesses of the human heart." Did we want the "same catastrophe" that had happened in Russia and they," must protect themselves against this kind of thing?" (23) The jury had no need to retire for their verdict. John MacLean was pronounced 'guilty' with the judge adding that MacLean was "Highly educated and intelligent" and knew what he was doing. The sentence was 5 years' imprisonment with MacLean turning to his supporters as he was led away shouting, "keep it going boys, keep it going."

This was a very historic moment. The war was coming to a close but MacLean was still a real and perceived threat to the British State. An alternative view of the world had been enunciated in a Scottish court room. It was no utopian meanderings. This view of the world was being fought for in other corners of Europe and America. The late Angus Calder summed up his speech from the dock as a:

"..national past and an international present intersected. Knox, Cameron and a legion of disposed clansmen stood behind him. So did the massed workers of Petrograd and Clydeside." (24)

This imagery of a national past and international present would swill around the mind of a man about to go into a third stint in prison; a man who, we have seen, was thinking about questions of personal identity and morality. In prison he was going to do this. MacLean wrote on Peterhead note paper (20/8/18) requesting a list of books and magazines citing that Bertrand Russell had this privilege. "If the same Act applies to Scotland as to England, so ought the treatment." He also requested the "concession" of a monthly visit and letter out and challenged the Government that if "they had nothing to hide or fear" then there was no case for preventing such intercourse with friends and family.

John MacLean with well-wishers outside the High Court in Edinburgh prior to the trial.

He listed 44 texts over the page that he required – all the Economics text books – Adam Smith, Alfred Marshall, Marx's Capital (Vol 2 and 3); standard history books of Greece, Italy, France, Germany and Russia; maths and geometry and the "poems of Shakespeare, Dryden, Pope, Keats, Shelley, Byron, William Morris, Bernard Shaw." All the cultural references of a British Socialist! No Scottish history, no Burns or Fergusson. In the authorities notes there is a memo rejecting a previous request with notes insinuating that hunger strike was being used as a tool to get what he wanted. In reply to the application on the 20th the Governor stated that he explained the No to MacLean and that the prisoner understood but would apply again.

Agnes, his wife, had no time to think about such things. She did have to contemplate visiting her husband with her young family in the north east again knowing that the journey from Pollokshaws to Peterhead wasn't – and still isn't – the easiest. She began a campaign for his release including letters to prominent politicians – her MP, George Barnes, the Labour leader, Ramsay MacDonald and many others. Her husband's hunger strike in October and brutal force feeding by prison staff was her utmost concern.

The wider Labour movement also mobilised. In the criminal papers there are original letters from trade union branches such as Calligraphers and Furnishers and Railwaymen, constituency Labour party branches as well as other Left organisations such as the ILP, BSP and the SLP. These letters came from Govan and Ipswich; Edinburgh and Portsmouth and lots of places in between. (25) At the Albert hall in London at a big Hands Off Russia rally there was a massive banner unfurled – **Release MacLean!** This was next to an equally massive banner that said **Hands off Russia!** A clear reference to the British Government's involvement in the Russian Civil War to topple the Bolshevik government. The lion tamer and socialist (and future MP) John S Clarke wrote a song called The Man in Peterhead:

"Then workers for your own sake - liberate MacLean! You could do it aye tomorrow if you dared.""

The Armistice was signed in November and the clamour for MacLean's release was growing. Not surprisingly there was no appetite among the authorities to release him but there was a prompt. In December there would be a General Election and the BSP had put forward MacLean's name as a Labour party candidate (as the BSP were technically affiliated to the Labour Party.) He had originally been nominated for the Birkenhead seat by Walton Newbold. However, he was accepted as a candidate in his own constituency of the Gorbals to take on his own MP, George Barnes. Willie Gallacher was to run the campaign on MacLean's behalf while he was in prison. This candidature would certainly raise MacLean's profile and it scared the authorities because a convicted felon could potentially get elected.

Probably to Agnes' surprise John was released in December just before the election. She would have hoped that he would take it easy. Well-wishers wrote to her with the best of intentions:

"I am so glad he is likely to get out and hope he will be strong again. He must leave the fight to others for a bit." (26)

If only headstrong politicos would listen to their wives and friends eh? MacLean was having none of this. He was released on a Free Pardon from George V himself. He was having none of this either. He wrote to the authorities on Boxing day asking for £150 compensation and claiming that Geordie, "should be in Holland with his cousin" and that it was the workers who had won him his freedom. (27)

In a memo of 9th December Munro considered what would happen if MacLean won the Gorbals seat and in his view MacLean should face disqualification as his conviction still stands and has not been annulled. Then again, what would happen if he was banned from taking his seat? The recent agitation would probably be repeated in an "apparated form, with the added accusation that the Government let him out well knowing that he could not sit…" (28) The Government were preparing for MacLean's possible election victory in the Gorbals by printing the list of disqualifications in his papers. The Act reads as relating to English law. The best Lord Clyde could muster was that although there "was no authority for it" he had no doubt that the common law of Scotland was the same as England's. (29) Clearly he didn't know and there was no Scottish precedent. Was this why they let him out? Hindsight tells us that MacLean polled over 7000 votes in the election and while Barnes won comfortably enough it is clear that MacLean commanded a considerable following. It would appear – rightly or wrongly – that with the war over John posed less of a threat out of prison than he would have posed as a convict MP.

With politics heating up over the water this was noted. Many Irish Republicans were still in prison and they were standing for election too including Eamon De Valera. MacLean's release was noted and used against the British Government. Many years later, Frank Gallagher who was a Cork born journalist and veteran Republican, wrote in his memoirs of the Irish Revolution:

"Then a formal demand was made on the British Government to set free the men who had been chosen as candidates that they might at least be able to conduct their campaign. A Scottish Communist was set free for the election in Britain, but the Irish must stay in jail." (30)

The ire was against Lloyd George and company and not the Scottish Communist. The proof of this can be seen if we travel back to 1918 to MacLean's pre-election hustings where something strange and significant occurred. The Scotsman reported:

"Mr. MacLean denied that he owed his release to Mr. Barnes. And said that the Highland spirit in him could never be crushed and he had come through the ordeal

loyal to his class and more bitter than ever against
capitalism and more determined to carry on the fight. He
described his release as a political dodge." (31)

At the same meeting a Dublin man spoke prior to his
arrival of the sympathy of Sinn Fein in Ireland with
MacLean. Where had this come from? MacLean said that he
would go to the Paris Peace Conference himself if
Woodrow Wilson did not release American political
prisoners. (32) Pieces of a strange jigsaw were falling
into place. A war that had begun wrapped in national
jingoism, in the nationalism of the empires, was now
ending with the national demands of those peoples around
Europe and beyond clamouring for national self-
determination. The internationalist and socialist
MacLean was talking about his "Highland spirit" and
being endorsed from the floor by Sinn Fein in Glasgow.
What was going on?

The MacLeans went on holiday doon the watter to
Rothesay. He didn't take the police officers - who were
watching him every day - on holiday with him. It wasn't
the done thing! He came back and let James Dodds (Under
Secretary of State) know that he and his wife were being
pestered by "detestable spies popularly called
detectives. I welcome their attention as it is a sign
that you are foaming at the mouth at having to release
me." (33)

John MacLean would come into conflict with the State
again and he knew he would. He would also come into
conflict with the British Left and nobody really saw
that coming.

NOTES

1) Quoted in David Howell, *A Lost Left - Three Studies in Socialism and Nationalism*, 1986, p. 187

2) Alexander Blok, The Twelve, January 1918 (translated from Russian by Maria Carlson), verse 3

3) John MacLean, *The war after the war in the light of working class economics.*, a pamphlet prepared for the 1917-18 Glasgow economics class, reprinted in *In the Rapids of Revolution*, 1978, p. 131

4) Ibid. p. 136

5) Nan Milton, *John MacLean*, 1973 p. 158.

6) John MacLean, Demand Petroff's release, The Call, 2/8/1917, in Jonson (ed) p. 254.

7) R Erskine of Mar, The Celtic and the Labour Movements, Guth na Bliadhna, An t-Earrach/Spring, 1918.

8) John MacLean papers, Acc 4251, National Library of Scotland, Edinburgh.

9) MacLean, *Letter to Georgy Chicherin*, 13/11/1917 in Jonson (ed), p. 260. The reference is to Chicherin's political past where some mud seems to have stuck!

10)   Milton, ibid. p. 156

11)   I am grateful to John Ford. I have this information from a talk given by John to the John MacLean Society on the activities of the IRA in the West of Scotland 1905 - 1923 where he touched on the situation in Lanarkshire.

12)   John MacLean criminal papers, HH16/132, Public records office, Edinburgh.

13)   Ibid.

14)   Ibid

15)   Ibid

16)   Witness testimonial in John Broom, *John MacLean*, 1973, p.110

17)   Alexander Blok, The Twelve, ibid, verse 9

18)   Accuser of Capitalism, John MacLean's speech from the dock, 9th May 1918, (edited by Terry Brotherstone), 1986, p. 15.

19)   Accuser of Capitalism, ibid, p. 20

20)   Accuser of Capitalism, ibid., p.31

21)   P.32

22)   P.36

23)   Lord Strathclyde summary in the John MacLean papers, Mitchell Library, Glasgow, TD260

24)   Angus Calder, *The Leader of the Glasgow Soviet*, Sunday Times Magazine, 25/11/1973. The Cameron referred to is the seventeenth century Presbyterian revolutionary, Richard Cameron.

25)   See the Criminal trial papers, HH16/132; HH16/133; HH16/134 in the Public Records Office, Edinburgh. It is worth noting that these letters were no flash in the pan due to the publicity around the case. The same branches wrote for his liberation during his stints in prison in 1921 also.

26)   An undated letter from W Manson (late 1918) in the MacLean papers, NLS, Acc 4251.

27)   MacLean Criminal papers, ibid. The Holland reference is to the Kaiser who fled Germany to sanctuary in Holland at the end of the war.

28)   Ibid.HH16/134

29)   David Hogan, The Four Glorious Years, 1953, p. 47. This was Gallagher's pseudonym. Gallagher opposed the Treaty with Britain that set up the Irish Free State and continued to hold to this Republican position.

30)   Ibid. HH16/133

31)   The Scotsman, 14/12/1918, in HH16/134.

32)   Glasgow Herald, 14/12/1918, Ibid

33)   HH16/134

**PART 2 – "Ireland will only get her republic when
Scotland gets hers."**

The conference was held in the Ancient Concert Rooms.
The BSP delegates left early. The occasion was a
skittish prank played by one of the Dubliners. A Union
jack was placed on the floor in place of a doormat.
Trampling on the symbol of the forcible fusion of
nations was more than the representatives of the
revolutionary proletariat could stomach….and out of the
conference arose the new 'Independent Labour Party of
Ireland.'

   - C Desmond Greaves (1)

James Connolly

Chapter 5 - All hail, The Scottish Workers Republic!

Scotland should go it alone Nan, and even then we'll not be that much alone. Why should Scottish lads have to die for John Bull in Ireland or anywhere else? It breaks my heart every time I read the War Casualty list in the Herald.

- Freddy Anderson (2)

Historians put the date at August 1920. In all that was happening within left wing and revolutionary politics in Britain John MacLean broke the mould. He broke from British socialism to be precise. It may have been logical to imagine that he would be a leading light with Willie Gallacher in the new Communist Party of Great Britain. MacLean did not comply. He called for a separate Scottish Communist Party and for Scottish independence. As he put it:

"Scotland must again have independence but not to be ruled by traitor kings or chiefs, lawyers or politicians." (3)

Scotland should be a republic: a workers' republic to be precise. This was truly revolutionary and it did not arise in a vacuum. As we shall see it was coming: the break with the CPGB, the emphasis on the Scottish national question consistent with his socialist politics.

MacLean put out 100,000 leaflets with the Tramp Trust Unlimited under the heading - **All hail, the Scottish Communist Republic!** Communist became Workers in time so as not to cause confusion with the Communist Party of GB. It was not a brilliantly written leaflet in the classic sense. Then again, for MacLean writing was a means to an end. MacLean was too busy agitating and educating to spend weeks on end scribbling away in the

Mitchell Library in Glasgow. It was, however, very powerful and put a Left alternative to what would become the British Road to Socialism although raw and clumsy in sections. It was rooted in its time contrary to what his many detractors would have us believe. I will explore the motivations and context in the next chapter but I will spend a little time exploring this remarkable leaflet.

The leaflet tried to do three things. Firstly, to put the case for Scottish independence. Secondly, to show a historical basis for this while keeping consistent with the communist push to take over the world and finally, John introduced his thoughts on Celtic communism. Quite a lot to cram into two A5 printed pages. It wasn't exactly the *Communist Manifesto* - Scottish style but it was a very powerful counterblast to the nascent Communist Party.

His thoughts on the national question had been forming for some time. He was involved in the debate around Scottish representation at the Paris Peace Conference in late 1918. I shall expand on this in the next chapter while emphasising for the moment the significance of post war developments. The war began with contending chauvinistic nationalisms that the Left failed to deal with. That same war ended with various national minorities raising their case for self-determination. The Left in Europe struggled with this too.

Scotland was affected by such calls which impacted on John MacLean. I sometimes feel that many on the Left over the years still feel that MacLean woke up one morning and in a mad fit came out for national independence! The Scottish Left had always been broadly pro-Home Rule. The Peace Conference gave a chance to raise this in a practical way.

Most significantly he was conversing with Gaelic nationalists and Irish socialists who couldn't separate the great Social Question from the National Question even if they had wanted to.

"For some time past the feeling has been growing that Scotland should strike out for national independence, as well as Ireland and other lands." (4)

John was capturing a mood – his mood – and a mood among sections of the Scottish Left. It was a Gaelic nationalist, Ruaraidh Erskine, who put it in historical context more eloquently than MacLean. Writing in the Winter of 1917 of the time when Scotland wakens up:

"This concealed agent or instrument exists and is fully potent unto national emancipation. No power on earth can deprive us of it. No power on earth can dispute the justness of our right to it, or gainsay us its use, if we wish to avail ourselves of it. It is Scottish history, revealed and consolidated in the one great fact of the sovereign independence of our country." (5)

A minority view in Scotland although a strong one in Ireland and Ireland would feature prominently from now until the end of his life. The War of Independence was in full swing and MacLean was aware of British atrocities from his visit to Ireland and news coming across the water from the Irish community in the west of Scotland. The most notorious being those of the Black and Tans – a collection of ex-soldiers, policemen and mercenaries so called for their part police, part army uniform. Scottish regiments had been prominent in the British presence in Ireland for a long time. Indeed, in 1913 the Kings Own Scottish Borderers notoriously fired on the crowd in Bachelor's Walk in Dublin. MacLean saw this as key:

"Genuine Scotsmen recently asked themselves the question: 'Are we Scots to be used as the bloody tools of the English against our brother Celts of Erin?'" (6)

Of course, not all Scots agreed. Many, then as now, had sons in the British Army and there was massive propaganda against IRA 'terrorism.' What really shook his former British Left comrades was the nationalist terminology. It was a new take on the old joke about the

Scotsman, the Englishman and the Irishman. Two of them had been divided for years by one's imperialism and they should wake up to it.

Are you laughing? No? The British Left didn't either.

Then there were our own Gaels. The treatment of the Land raiders on Lewis had aroused those from the Highlands and Islands on Clydeside. The "filthy tactics" of Lord Leverhulme and his actions in dismissing workers in Stornoway who had shown solidarity with the Lewis land raiders who had seized land and started building houses in Coll and Gress were cited as another example of divide and conquer. This was capitalism – English capitalism denying ex-servicemen who had been promised crofts at the end of the war. His old Left pals would not see any distinction. Capitalism was capitalism as far as they were concerned.

This analysis was based on events in Lewis in 1920 concerning the land raiders and the divide and conquer tactics of the island's owner. Lord Leverhulme had amassed his fortune from soap. In characteristic fashion this knighted, wannabee aristocrat had bought himself a Scottish island. Two islands actually as he bought the conjoined isles of Lewis and Harris in 1917. Leverhulme talked big. He would bring industry and jobs to Stornoway and develop farming and fish farming on the island. At the end of the War many soldier Gaels returned to the Highlands and islands expecting the land 'fit for heroes' as Lloyd George famously put it. Instead they had to resort to the old tactic of land raiding. 30 or so soldiers occupied farms in Coll and Gress near Back on Lewis to make their stand.

Gael mobilised the Tramp Trust. Sandy Ross visited the Gress raiders during the Glasgow Fair in July. MacLean set off on 2nd August after returning from Dublin and gave his account of events in the Vanguard. (7) He visited the Coll raiders although most of them were away at the fishing. John mentioned his speech at a meeting in Stornoway but not that he spoke with some ILP comrades at an event organised by the Highland Land League. This group were a radical organisation who brought together various strands of the Scottish radical tradition and whose meetings combined socialist speeches, calls for Home Rule and/or Independence, land reform and some Gaelic psalms. (8) They had branches in Glasgow, Paisley, Greenock and even London. MacLean was exposed to this. They even finished all meetings emulating the Irish Manchester Martyrs with the cry – **God Save Scotland!**

If the Stornoway Gazette is to be believed then MacLean's intervention was massively unpopular and out of touch with feeling on the island. It is true that many workers in Stornoway itself blamed the land raiders for Leverhulme's suspension of employment opportunities in the town. The crofters' position was put to Leverhulme in 1919 at a meeting:

"You have bought this island but you have not bought us and we refuse to be bond slaves of any man. We want to live our lives in our own way, poor in material things it may be but at least it will be free of the factory bell; it will be free and independent." (9)

The rich businessman wouldn't have understood this view and neither did the Stornoway proletariat. MacLean wanted the crofters to hold firm and was frustrated by the lack of solidarity between town and country. Yet it was Gaelic independence and freedom and this was what the ex-servicemen were asserting. To be fair to MacLean he had supported the crofters' struggles back in his Gael column reporting on land raids from Sutherland to Lewis and criticising the actions of the aristocrats and the Liberal Government. Back in 1913 he wrote in relation to another Lewis raid:

"Since the raid by the Uig crofters in Lewis, the Board of Agriculture has somewhat awakened from its slumber, and is promising holdings in

four parishes - shortly. It is a pity that the
Gaels of Scotland have not the fire and go of
the Celts of Ireland, whose dare-devil
determination has gained holdings and houses
for them. Strange though it may seem to many
city dwellers, the Highland huts are in many
respects inferior to the caves of prehistoric
man a hundred thousand years ago on this spot
on the planet. That is what capitalist,
Liberal and Tory, politicians call progress.
Light now begins to dawn on us as to their
surprise at Highland depopulation. We trust
that this Uig raid will be the precursor of a
Gaelic movement to clear all landlords out of
the Highlands." (10)

For the local rag, MacLean was the "antithesis" of all
that patriotic Lewis men should be. (11) Although
painting the Glasgow socialist as an unwanted outsider
does not sit with MacLean's consistent support for the
crofters over a good few years. There is a real passion
that resonates in his call for a Gaelic movement to free
the Highlands from landlordism allied with his call for
the Scottish Gael to learn from the Irish Celt. By his
own admission he had returned from Dublin which he had
visited to, "establish an entente between the Celts of
Scotland and the Celts of Ireland and to further my
efforts to prevent Scottish boys being used by England
to murder Irish boys." (12) Passions that were
suppressed in a wider British Socialist movement were
set free at the end of WW1 as Gael returned to his
roots. A proper reading of John MacLean or if you care
painting the whole portrait should take the surprise out
of the appearance of this remarkable leaflet with its
call for a Scottish Workers' Republic.

The poor old Stornoway Gazette reported on how 250 attended a meeting back in Glasgow chaired by Angus MacDonald of the HLL addressed by the "antithesis" himself. It is quite humorous to read the report of MacLean's call for solidarity from Stornoway's workers with the ex- servicemen:

"As a paradox this takes some beating: there must be no wage earners on Lewis, yet a Dictatorship of wage earners is to rule the great Commune which this hare brained creature advocates. So that rules Lewis out of any 'ruling' that is to be done."

The author also ended with the rallying cry of God Save Scotland…" from malcontents, extremists etc." (13) The report railed against his criticism back in Glasgow of the crofters' submission.

In November MacLean reported on the defeat of the raiders in the Vanguard blaming their lawyer, Donald Shaw, for advising the raiders to give up their occupation. "It looks as if the people had sold their sons' very lives for a mess of pottage…." (14) To be fair MacLean does come across as quite embittered that the crofters had not taken his advice.

As a postscript the compromise of 1920 did not last. Neither Leverhulme nor the Government were able to follow through on any promises made. By June 1921 the farms were raided again which set in place a chain of events that led to the Government updating their land settlement scheme and creating 57 new holdings and the Treasury agreeing to sanction £10,069 for these new holdings in Galson and Leverhulme's opposition was overruled as the 'district is dangerous.' This all happened in January 1923. (15) It was a victory of sorts but not for the island in general. Leverhulme's big talk was just that. As James Hunter wrote of the failure of the Soap lord's proposal for fishing development:

"Hence the re-enactment in Stornoway, in April 1923, of scenes reminiscent of those a century before – with several hundred people setting sail on a single ship, the Metagama, for North America." (16)

The isles could not afford another haemorrhaging of people on this scale.

The monument to the land raiders in Gress on the Isle of Lewis.

For MacLean, however, as he penned his leaflet in August 1920 English capitalism was at work in the Highlands and Islands of Scotland and as the leaflet goes on to explain, this was the way it had been for a long time. 1707, 1715 and 1745 were cited. To Scottish nationalists this was staple fare. John MacLean ventured into fairly new terrain. Edinburgh lawyers and politicians had sold out Scotland in 1707. The Jacobite rebellions were reactions against this. The clan chiefs became "Englishmen in outlook" and sold out their people and it was the dispossessed Highlanders who became the cannon fodder of the new English empire. The Highland Clearances get mentioned too.

It was a whistle stop tour of Scottish history from someone who had been getting a crash course, as we shall see, from left Scottish nationalists. As we have touched on, those same Scot nats, including William Gillies, had rightly criticised MacLean in 1916 when his beloved Scottish Labour College was founded. The Scottish Review criticised, "the absence of any definite place for the study of Scottish history from the national and democratic point of view." (17) English, algebra, Industrial history, Marxian scholars would all be studied but there was not a single mention of Scottish history. Willie Gallacher, Manny Shinwell and other British socialists must have read this crash course in Scottish history with utter bewilderment. They drew a conclusion, as history has told us.

The final part of the leaflet outlines his path to a workers' republic. Ireland and Russia were the inspiration. His left nationalist pals had been teaching him about Celtic communism (just like James Connolly had been taught too.) Celtic communism as a notion would have been attractive to Celtic communists wouldn't it? It seems quaint to modern readers and would not get much discussion time among modern left wing thinkers in Scotland as I write in 2016 but that is not the point. It was influential.

Again it is worth pondering on the fact that his pal Erskine of Mar brought this concept to his attention. Erskine had a few languages under his belt and was aware of the later work of Frederick Engels in looking at primitive communist societies. (18) It probably would not have been widely available in translated English form at that time. Erskine was aware of it and published a couple of articles under the title, *Celtic Tribal Communism* in MacLean's Vanguard newspaper in 1920. It was no fad though because MacLean had it re-printed by

the Socialist newspaper in Winter 1922-3. Erskine
believed that Engels' work proved that, "the human race
was cradled in communism." (19) He elaborated on Engels'
analysis of Celtic society by explaining the origin of
the clans giving examples including the MacLeans in Mull
which may have pleased his pal. What is striking is that
in the various attempts of the left in Scotland to
explain Scottish history they couldn't see the role of
the British State in the final suppression of that
society. Erskine's article shows how important the
defeat at Culloden and the Clearances were to the
cementing of the British State. (20)

This was hugely influential. Karl Marx had written of
the clearance of areas as large as German principalities
in the Gaeltachd. Marx wrote passionately of the
treatment of the Gael at the hands of their chiefs -
primarily the Countess of Sutherland - and the British
soldiers who carried out the evictions. (21) Yet there
is not a single word about this in MacLean's lecture
notes on Capital. The Scottish Labour College was the
poorer for it. It took a Scottish nationalist to
enlighten him to such issues.

He was duly enlightened. A National Council must be set
up in Glasgow with various district councils feeding in
and control would rest with the workers - male and
female alike:

"The country must have but one clan as it were - a
united people working in cooperation and cooperatively
using the wealth that is created." (22)

There is no denying that this was not a nationalist
leaflet. His socialism underpinned this leaflet and he
was attempting to make the demand for independence
consistent with the ideology that was going to change
the world. He saw no contradiction. This was before
communism was tainted even in the eyes of most of the
Left by the same Bolsheviks who John supported. His
language of a people working in cooperation and
cooperatively is not the sole preserve of communists.

97

The early Disciples of Christ huddled in a room;
Levellers in England in the seventeenth century, the New
Lanark experiment and French socialist thinkers in the
early nineteenth century as well as a young Charlie Marx
saw this as the natural way of organising society.
MacLean had been in the socialist army all his life and
had no intentions of leaving it. He could never have
foreseen what was to come in the name of communism.

What is really revolutionary in this leaflet is that it
reinforces the orthodoxy - Marxism and the dictatorship
of the working class while challenging the orthodox -
the Marxists themselves. Quite clever really and is
absolutely as important as his speech from the dock in
1918 in defining who he was and is to us today. In an
article in the Vanguard entitled *Irish Stew* shortly
after he summed this up quite succinctly:

"If the Bolshevik notion of world communism through
national communism is scientifically correct, then we
are justified in utilising our latent Highland and
Scottish sentiments and traditions in the mighty task
confronting us of transforming capitalism into
communism." (23)

For years the British left explained this away.
Trotskyist organisations as well as the CPGB
rationalised this as the product of defeat. Had the
Revolution succeeded in 1919 would MacLean have even
mentioned Scotland and independence? To be fair it is an
interesting question but utterly irrelevant. If he had
been a good fitba' player would he have played for
Queens Park? If the Clydeside MP's had done a Sinn Fein
and stayed at home would this have vindicated MacLean's
position and created some space for revolutionary
politics in Scotland? If, if, if.

What we do know is those latent Highland and Scottish
sentiments had been stirring in him once again from
before the defeat of the Revolution in Western Europe.
Too many forget this about MacLean. It is a human
explanation that I see in his call for a Scottish

Workers Republic in August 1920 not a sophisticated
Marxist analysis of a defeat.

All Hail, the Scottish

Workers' Republic!

(First published, Aug., 1920.)

Reprinted

For some time past the feeling has been growing that Scotland should strike out for National Independence, as well as Ireland and other lands. This has recently been strengthened by the English Government's intention to rely mainly on Scottish troops to murder the Irish race.

Genuine Scotsmen recently asked themselves the question: "Are we Scots to be used as the bloody tools of the English against our brother Celts of Erin?" And naturally the instinctive response was—No!

Again, the land seizures by Highland crofters is arousing the blood of Highlanders driven south to the Clyde Valley for work. Especially the filthy tactics of Lord Leverhulme (an English capitalist), who has dismissed Stornoway wage-slaves as a means of beating the Lewis raiders who seized the farms of Coll and Gress. Divide and conquer again!

Interest in the Highland land question has again been roused, and students are re-reading the Highland clearances.

Scottish students of history now realise that Edinburgh lawyers and politicians sold Scottish Independence in 1707, although most blame has fallen on the Earl of Stair. Many of us are convinced that ever since 1707 the Edinburgh kings' and queens' counsels and politicians have been in the regular pay of London to keep Scotland as the base tool of the English Government. These scoundrels in the eighteenth century helped to ruin Burns, the peasants' and people's poet.

The "Rebellions" of 1715 and 1745 were natural reactions against the treacherous deed of 1707, but these unfortunate outbursts but gave the English the excuse and chance to subdue the Highland chiefs, and then corrupt them with an English education at Oxford or Cambridge.

Since 1750 the chiefs became Englishmen in outlook, and used their clansmen to defend English capitalism against the Revolution started in Paris in 1789. Since the Napoleonic wars Highland regiments have been used to defend the stolen lands of England all over the globe, and have largely helped to extend the English Empire.

Whilst doing this, the Dukes of Sutherland and Argyll and

other chiefs proceeded with the English landlord policy of land clearances. The friends of the fighters were chased off their native heath into the lowlands or out to Canada and Australia.

Now the reaction is beginning — inspired by Ireland and Russia.

Scotland must again have Independence, but not to be ruled by traitor kings and chiefs, lawyers and politicians. The Communism of the clans must be re-established on a modern basis. (Bolshevism, to put it roughly, is but the modern expression of the Communism of the Mir.) Scotland must therefore work itself into a Communism embracing the whole country as a unit. The country must have but one clan, as it were—a united people working in co-operation and co-operatively, using the wealth that is created.

We can safely say, then: Back to Communism and Forward to Communism.

The control must be in the hands of the workers only, male and female alike, each workshop and industry sending delegates to District Councils and the National Council.

The National Council must be established in or near Glasgow, as half the population lives within a radius of twenty miles from Glasgow.

In the period of transition a Wage-earners' Dictatorship must guide production, and the adoption of the machinery and methods of production, to Communist methods.

Many Irishmen live in Scotland, and, as they are Celts like the Scots, and are out for Irish Independence, and as wage-earners have been champion fighters for working-class rights, we expect them to rally themselves with us, and help us to attain our Scottish Communist Republic, as long as they live in Scotland. Irishmen must remember that Communism prevailed amongst the Irish clans as amongst the Scottish clans, so that, in lining up with Scotsmen, they are but carrying forward the traditions and instincts of the Celtic Race.

All Hail the Scottish Workers' Republic!

JOHN MACLEAN, M.A.

The leaflet that defined MacLean's stance on Scottish independence and his break with British socialism. This contemporary version went out with his General Election leaflet in the Gorbals in 1922. (Source: Gallacher Memorial Library)

NOTES

(1)   C Desmond Greaves, *The Life and Times of James Connolly*, 1986 edn, p. 278. The BSP is the British Socialist Party.

(2)   Freddy Anderson, *Krassivy: A Play about the Great Socialist, John MacLean*, 2005, p.70

(3)   John MacLean, *In the Rapids of Revolution*, 1978, p. 218.

(4)   MacLean, Ibid, p. 217

(5)   R Erskine of Marr, *Ireland and Scotland at the Peace Congress*, The Scottish Review, Vol 40, Winter 1917, p. 418-9.

(6)   MacLean, Ibid, p.217

(7)   The Highland Land Seizures, September, 1920 in MacLean ibid, 222

(8)   Iain Fraser Grigor, *Highland Resistance: The Radical Tradition in the Scottish North*, 2000, p. 185

(9)   See Madeleine Bunting, Cumhachd do na Daoine: Gaelic the Secret Language of Revolution, Sunday Herald, 25/09/2016, p.29. The Gaelic translates as Power to the People.

(10)   Gael, Justice, 13/12/1913 p.6

(11)   The Stornoway Gazette, 13/8/1920.

(12)   MacLean, ibid, p.222

(13)   The Stornoway Gazette, 27/8/1920.

(14)   Stray Straws: the defeat of the Raiders, November 1920, MacLean, ibid, p.224. See also Ian Mitchell, A Bolshevik's Visit to Lewis between the wars, West Highland Free Press, 29/5/1995. Mitchell makes some very perceptive comments but is not aware of MacLean's long standing interest in crofting matters.

(15)   See Ewen A Cameron, *Land for the People? The British Government and the Scottish Highlands c.1880 - 1925*, 1996 p. 176

(16)   James Hunter, *Last of the Free: A History of the Highlands and Islands of Scotland*, 1999, p.341

(17)   James D Young, *The Rousing of the Scottish Working Class*, 1979, p.195

(18)   *The Origin of the Family, Private Property
        and the State*, in Marx/Engels, *Selected Works in
        One Volume*, 1968, p. 545
(19)   Ruaraidh Erskine of Marr, *The Socialist*,
        December 1922 (John MacLean supplement)
(20)   Erskine of Marr, *The Socialist*, January 1923.
(21)   Karl Marx, *Capital*, Vol 1, 1954 edition, p.
        683.
(22)   MacLean, Ibid, p 218.
(23)   MacLean, Ibid, p.219.

Chapter 6 – A middle aged man looks at the Thistle

I felt it turn and syne I saw

John Knox and Clavers in my raw,

and Mary Queen o' Scots ana',

and Rabbie Burns and Weelum Wallace

and Carlyle lookin' unco gallus

and Harry Lauder to enthral us….

They cannae learn sae canne move,

But stick for aye to their auld groove

-   The only race in history who've
    Bidden in the same category
    Frae start to present o' their story
    And deem their ignorance their glory.

-   Hugh MacDiarmid (1)

MacLean had an awareness of his identity that was
specifically Scottish.

-   David Howell (2)

Do you know what Ahma means? Those familiar with Stanley
Baxter's great intellectual study – Parliamo Glasgow –
will remember that it is a statement of identity. Ahma
means "I'm a" in Glaswegian. Ahma chancer; Ahma pure
genius; Ahma nashernalist and so on. (3) Personal
identity in eloquent Glaswegian.

Identity can also be the dark art of politics. Indeed,
when people talk about identity politics something
dangerous is assumed – race or racialism. Yet doesn't
personal identity infuse a lot of what we do? The older
you get the more these questions come to the fore. We
challenge who we are, what we were and think about what

we can be in the limited time we have left on this planet.

For some it might be the abandonment of career and a new direction in their lives. For more still it might mean a crisis of faith or belief. Or I suppose it can also be going back to roots, the first principles of who we are about. It is the most personal thing and we all have our own individual way of capturing this. You don't have to be sitting down and consciously thinking about it to be thinking about it!

I am certainly no expert and definitely no psychologist but I find it fascinating.

Jim Young once told me how he had discovered that Leon Trotsky was rediscovering his Jewish identity in his later years before he was murdered in Mexico in 1940. Then there is James Connolly. His participation in the Easter Rising totally confused the British Left. Walter Kendall cites the fact that the British Socialist Party Easter Conference in 1916 heard no emergency resolutions on the situation in Dublin even though the Conference was in session while the Green Flag was flying over the city. (4) This is quite incredible that the main socialist organisation in Britain should not even discuss the rebellion in which Connolly's Irish Citizen Army should play such a huge part.

While the British executions of the leaders were taking place, Tom Johnston in the *Forward* expressed his puzzlement that Connolly could take part in a "futile" rising that could never lead to a socialist Ireland. (5) Only the Catholic Socialist Notes column (John Wheatley's group) saluted the brave men and condemned the executions. (6) Not to labour the point, even as late as 1919, Arthur McManus (a friend of Connolly) seemed as if he was justifying his old friend to the socialist world. Yet while making the case that Connolly died a revolutionary socialist, McManus wrote that the transformation from anti-militarist to Commandant of the Citizen Army was:

"..a problem for psychology, perplexing to even the most diligent, but uninformed observer and here let me state to no one more than the present writer, as many in Dublin know." (7)

Connolly explained it all in one powerful phrase: "They will all forget," he said, "that I am an Irishman." It didn't negate any of his socialist politics or his vision for a workers' republic. It just explained why during wartime he decided to fight for Ireland along with the Sinn Feiners. This personal identity had been there through most of his writings as the boy from an Irish Catholic ghetto in the Cowgate in Edinburgh grappled with issues of politics, faith and nationality through most of his political life. In middle age he didn't need to grapple any more. He was socialist and he was Irish. And he made his Confession and received Holy Communion before he was executed.

This is not a compare and contrast study between MacLean and Connolly. But there is a lesson here as I think about John MacLean. It is my belief as I read and re-read some of MacLean's writings that identity played on his mind. Many things facilitated this - War; his own past, his association with left nationalists and the dual cultural traditions of the Scottish Left. We shall look at these in turn as they are key to understanding the latter part of John MacLean's life. This is not original as they have come out in other biographies of MacLean. But the point is that they were facilitators of some key changes in John's politics but they were not the root cause. It may not be earth shattering to some but it is my contention that a middle aged man, who had been through the wars, was thinking about who and what he was.

MacLean's parents were part of a strong Glasgow Gaelic community. The language was spoken in the house. We know that he was of the MacLeans of Mull and went to the Original Secession Church when he was younger. As Ian Mitchell pointed out English was the language of progress for the children and there is no evidence that MacLean had the language (8) Yet it was no artistic flick that MacLean contributed to the *Justice* newspaper before the War under the pseudonym, Gael.

Now 'Gael' was a convinced, loyal British Socialist who took the Party line. Yet his column argued in 1912 that a Scottish parliament was a "distinct possibility" and it should be utilised as a machine for democracy. More powerfully he compared the British Party with the Westminster Parliament:

"It is bad enough for Parliament to alot only a day and a half to Scotland; it is worse still to have a British Socialist Executive without a representative from Scotland." (9)

This was way before his interest in the Scottish national question took an upturn in 1918. They are sporadic comments but they show the awareness, the identity, was there. Few things just happen out of serendipity. There is usually background and context. A perusal of the Independent Labour Party's *Forward* newspaper shows this Jekyll and Hyde approach to identity and cultural questions. They were a Scottish Left in a British Party. This duality weighed heavily. To be socialist, to be international, in their context meant cross border solidarity with workers in England, Wales and Ireland. The Irish Left saw through this.as MacLean would come to see through it too. You don't have to be subsumed in an Anglo-centric party to prove your internationalist credentials. Poor, old Forward didn't. This was summed up for me by a series of articles on Scottish history by J O'Connor Kessock way back in 1907. Concluding an article on the 1820 Rising in Scotland the ILPer concluded:

" The day is near when the final struggle will take place between oppressors and oppressed. Not on the wild hills of Bonnymuir but on the floor of the House of Commons." (10)

Such history and culture permeated the newspaper and the Scottish left. Its idiom was Scottish but its aspiration was a British road to Socialism. MacLean himself made similar comments on Scottish history in his Gael column. The analogy of a Scottish left within a British party applied as much to the BSP. Of course after his own death in 1923 the ILP would become a north British Left within a British party but the Labour Party had a journey before it got to that stage. Through that journey they would still be Jekyll and Hyde on Scottish cultural issues.

War had an impact. Of course in 1914 all nationalism was the same to the Left. The workers and their political parties would stand firm against national chauvinism. Then, " A God took revenge whose existence was denied." (11) We have seen how the major social democratic parties voted to support their national governments. MacLean's socialist internationalism marked out his stand against this imperialist war. He never lost this internationalism but something was changing.

Forward took an admirable line in opposing the slaughter from a pacifist viewpoint but a different discourse was taking place. Left nationalists were questioning the logic in the Letters columns. In November 1914 H C MacNeacail questioned the ILP policy on Home Rule as not going far enough. (12) The Scots were less conservative than the English and the break-up of the UK must be a spinoff of the War. Such thinking was winning over the Scottish Left especially as the war progressed.

By Winter 1917 a Scottish trade union - the Associated Iron moulders of Scotland - called a national protest. In line with Irish aspirations this protest was to call for Scottish representation at any International peace congress:

"..(point 2) Protest against the pretended right of England to appear and speak in name, and on behalf, of Scotland at any International Congress." (13)

These are just a couple of examples but plough through the *Forward* at this time and you will see more. A different type of nationalism based on the demand for national self-determination (be that home rule or independence) was emerging out of the carnage of a British Empire entangled in a futile world war. Across the water in Ireland the Left and the Republicans opposed the war from the start. The socialists took the same international position but as war went on they saw the potential of the break-up of the UK and the forces of the Crown. Connolly and the socialist Irish Citizen Army draped the famous banner from Liberty Hall – **We Serve Neither King nor Kaiser but Ireland.** Not the international working class but Ireland. Had the same 'god' took its revenge again?

Scotland was not Ireland in 1916. MacLean and the Left kept the Party line as loyal British socialists. The dialogue was changing as the war came to a close. Within Forward and the Labour party in general debates were taking place around Scotland and her place in the UK, and the world, at the end of the war. Left nationalists were driving some of these discussions in those letters to *Forward*, in those petitions to trade unions and the wider population. They too had condemned the war and they wanted something positive to come out of it – the break-up of empires.

MacLean was approached in 1918 to sign a petition for Scottish representation at the Paris Peace Conference. He was part of the dialogue. He sympathised but didn't sign saying that the Bolsheviks were the true friends of Scottish Home Rule and not Woodrow Wilson. By 1919 he had joined changed his tune and joined Marr's National Committee and within a year and a half he was seconding a motion to a meeting of the Highland Land League in Glasgow calling for independence," with an explanation that he was out for a Scottish Communist Republic. Their independent Scotland would be ruled by the men from the workshops, the fishing boats and from the land. Glasgow would be their centre and not Edinburgh, the English capital of Scotland." (14) Roland Muirhead, socialist and member of the Scottish Home Rule Association (SHRA) had moved the motion and politely re-joined that that would be a matter for the people of Scotland.

A couple of months before his revolutionary leaflet MacLean had come out for Scottish independence. This didn't happen in a vacuum but arose out of real debates among progressive voices in Scotland. James Hunter has written of a flirtation between the Labour Party and the Highland Land League. There were joint candidates in crofting constituencies; they supported the advancement of Gaelic; they both believed that Scottish workers were more politically progressive and that the ownership of land and resources should belong to what Forward called, "the Scottish State." (15)

This was a real debate within Labour and socialist circles. What part should Home Rule or independence (the terms were interchangeable) play in the struggle for socialist change? John came out from his third stint in prison in late 1918 and stood as a Labour Party candidate in the Gorbals in the post war General Election. He was privy to these debates. A man who had been in prison three times for sedition, for his belief in a social revolution, saw the terms of the debate changing.

The nationalists of the Left were plugging away. In various journals such as Liberty and Guth na Bliadhna (Voice of the Year) leading left Scottish nationalists were saying the same things and more. Ruaraidh Erskine of Marr was one such voice who was influenced by and influenced John MacLean. In 1918 his Guth na Bliadhna had raised the three creeds of the 'Celtic Movement': national self-determination; land for the people; native language and culture. (16) Furthermore he claimed to have the support of Robert Smillie, the Scottish leader of the Miners Union who claimed that organised labour were behind our movement.

Ruaraidh was born in Brighton, raised in Edinburgh and learned the Gaelic language fluently from his nanny. (17) His journey had taken him from the SHRA to pan-Gaelic nationalism. He was generally supportive of the Russian Revolution and as we have seen was praising Engels views on kinship and the clan system. There is no doubting MacLean's influence here. Yet, for Erskine the cause of the Gael, the crofter in Scottish terms should not be ignored by the urban revolutionaries.

This was consistent with what the crofters told Leverhulme in 1919 as he tried to buy them and their island. By 1921 he was becoming more critical of the Marxist position on rural issues:

" Tha baile agus dùthaich ann, is iad le chèile a' stri gu searbh mu'n bhuaidh. Air ceann nan cathair is nam baile, tha luchd-leanmhuinn Kharl Marx, ach na tuath is an cairdean, is beag orra Karl Marx, is mar sin cha bhi cuid no gnothach aca ris-san no ris na deisciobuil a dh'fhag e ' na dheidh." (18)

This was based on what he saw happening in Russia post Revolution with the farmers. In the previous issue Erskine had written that Marx's words on the countryside poor were empty:

"Grathann beag air ais, is biodh luchd na dùthcha a' sireadh rain daibh fèin air luchd nam baile; ach ged a shir cha d'fhuair iad riamh dad a chur an acrais a bh' orra an lasachadh ach clach-bholg de'n bhòilsich aig Karl Marx. Is marbh Karl Marx, ach air mhaireann than a soisgeul Ceiltich." (19)

" SCOTTISH REVIEW" ISSUE 42 - 1919

Chronicles of the Quarters.

The National Committee.

The composition of the new National Committee is as follows :

> JOSEPH F. DUNCAN, General Secretary, Farm Servants' Union.
>
> DUNCAN MACGREGOR GRAHAM, M.P.
>
> WILLIAM GRAHAM, M.P.
>
> J. M. HOGGE, M.P.
>
> THOMAS JOHNSTON, Editor of *Forward*.
>
> Councillor DAVID KIRKWOOD.
>
> ANGUS MACDONALD, President, Comunn an Fhearainn, (The Highland Land League).
>
> AONGHAS MAC EANRUIG, Editor of *Alba*.
>
> JOHN MACLEAN, M.A.
>
> NEIL MACLEAN, M.P.
>
> JAMES MAXTON, M.A.
>
> JOHN ROBERTSON, M.P.
>
> ROBERT SMILLIE, President, Miners' Federation.
>
> ALEXANDER WILKIE, M.P.
>
> RUARAIDH ARASCAIN IS MHAIRR.

It will be within the recollection of our readers that the original committee was formed in order to present to the late Congress of Versailles the case of Scotland for separate representation at that gathering. Doubtless, it will also be within the recollection of our readers that a Memorial, setting forth the Scottish claim to separate representation at the Peace Conference, was drawn up, which document, we may now add, was sent to President Poincairé, who acknowledged its receipt, but took, apparently, no further steps in that matter. Thus were the anticipations of the original Committee realised, which of the camouflaged fig-tree of Versailles expected not anything so entirely foreign to its nature as a specimen of our national emblem. To change the figure somewhat, and our point of view also, let no man accuse us of now finding those grapes sour which we knew from the first to be charged with all bitterness, and unfit to be eaten even of pigs.

447

MacLean supported Marr's National Committee contrary to Broom's view in his biography.

111

MacLean had always been one of the 'luchd-leanmhuinn Kharl Marx' and the challenge was taken to him. The petition for Paris in 1918 was an example as was his visit to Lewis two years later as a sort of response. MacLean would have probably taken one almighty huff had he been able to translate Ruaraidh's criticism of his hero. Although to be fair, there is an echo in Erskine's critique of the reasons as to why there should be joint work between the HLL and the Labour party,

In mid-1919 MacLean joined Erskine's National Committee which also comprised Bob Smillie, David Kirkwood, Tom Johnston and Jimmy Maxton among others. It is quite amazing that such prominent Labour Party members could be in this Committee advocating the restoration of national self-determination and this fact has been wiped from our history books and it backs the point that this was no isolationist position adopted by MacLean but one that was common among the left in Scotland at the end of the war. Characteristically John was to the left and first started calling for a "communist republic" from mid-1919. (20)

There was a wider nationalist critique and Erskine kept plugging away at MacLean. He fostered a relationship that entailed contributing to each other's newspapers. In time MacLean would join Erskine's Scots Natiqnal League culminating in him chairing a meeting in Arbroath in 1920 to commemorate the 600th anniversary of the famous Declaration of Independence. He praised the editor of Liberty, John MacArthur who edited the best paper, "from a Scots standpoint" and was teaching, "true Scots history instead of the false and perverted variety taught in the school books." (21) Another motion was passed supporting the restoration of a "sovereign nation."

This is key. In the pages of Liberty MacLean read about the '45, Thomas Muir, the United Scotsmen and the 1820 Rising from a completely different standpoint. We have seen the duality of identity with the treatment of history in Forward. There was no such duality with the Liberty newspaper which had radicalised itself from the 'Scottish Home Rule Journal' to 'the Scottish National Journal' with the alluring sub heading of 'Enlightened nationalism is the basis of true internationalism.' These events in Scottish history were all pieces in a jigsaw – a great struggle for Scottish freedom with social struggle at its heart. In other words, the Scottish radical tradition.

From a Scottish labour college 4 years earlier which made no mention of Scottish history, MacLean's eyes were opened. Some of his critics in 1916 were now his educators. William Gillies was one such. (22) He wrote in November 1920 in relation to the failure of the Scottish national convention in the 1790's:

"So the Convention went down. The Scottish Republic is dead. Long live the Scottish Republic that is to be!" (23)

Does it sound familiar? Only a couple of months before, sure, wasn't MacLean hailing a Scottish Republic to be? It's just that he wanted the Workers to run it. The language is too similar. MacLean's Vanguard newspaper throughout 1920 had been critical of British imperialism in Ireland and India. So too had Liberty. This, more than the language or the cultural issues, hooked MacLean and he explored how this imperialism had cut its teeth in Scotland in the Gàidhealtachd, in suppressing the early Scottish democracy in the late eighteenth century and by re-writing our history. Like minds who wanted an independent Scotland, out of the British Empire, were talking about a cooperative commonwealth, Russia and internationalism.

There have been many debates around this part of John MacLean's life. For my part I believe that he got older and was thinking a lot – as we all do – about himself. A middle aged man looked at the thistle, to paraphrase Hugh MacDiarmid's poem, in line with who he was at that point in time. He never left the socialist army but he

did start to ask the great National Question as many
factors jolted at who he was. His latent Highland and
Scottish sentiments did not take him off in any new
direction if we look hard enough. It is true that
superficially he abandoned British socialism and looked
for a Scottish road to socialism but wasn't this the
heart of the Scottish socialist movement anyway? And
wasn't this heart suppressed to accommodate socialist
change across Britain? 'Gael' just started to think
about Scotland, her history, her role in Britain's
empire and her contribution to making this world better
for all the working class. It is worth remembering that
while Kirkwood and Johnston would abandon earlier
thoughts of a national committee in Scotland, MacLean
stayed true to his Republic.

My thoughts are strengthened by the fact that MacLean
just took this position as read. He did not develop any
new theories or write extensively on Scottish history.
He still had the same interests as he had when he was an
orthodox British socialist in the Classics, economics
and English poetry yet he stayed true to his Republic
until death. He was socialist and he was Scottish. It
was who he was and his post war politics moulded and
shaped around this.

Gael had come home.

It was in vogue for Marxists at the time to wax lyrical
on the National Question. Treatises, essays and books
torturing themselves as to the position that class
conscious workers and socialists should adopt on nations
and nationalism. Connolly, Lenin, Stalin and Otto Bauer
in Austria all weighed in. My old friend Donald Anderson
always taught me Lenin's maxim that there was a
nationalism of the oppressed and a nationalism of the
oppressor. Yet there was no such theoretical or
intellectual workout from MacLean. This was not just
because he was not an extensive writer because he still
wrote on the key things that mattered to him and he did
focus on the Scottish national question in the later

years of his life. To read these articles and the quotes from them so far (and to come) is to see someone who took his identity and the political course of action as read. There was no need to justify a separate Scottish party because logic dictated that this should be the course of action for Scottish Communists.

A good example of this was MacLean's reprinting of an English language Bolshevik pamphlet, *Russia's Appeal to Britain's Workers* in August 1920. This was the same time as he was coming out for a Scottish Workers Republic and falling out massively with the new Communist Party. MacLean calmly used his Preface to call for a Communist Council of Action to be based in Glasgow leading to a separate Scottish Party based in the same city. Russia still needed support and Scottish workers were in a better place to give this support. Now you could pick faults with this line of argument but there was not a lot of theory to pick fault with. He didn't feel it necessary. It was logical, a wee bit Calvinist and thoroughly in line with a middle aged man's view of the world.

Nor was his support for independence some tactical, political intervention from a defeated revolutionary as some would have us believe. They don't get the part that is not in any political manual or manifesto. They all forget that he was Scottish. In an excellent piece on 'the British superstition' in October, Erskine was to pre-empt what MacLean would find with his experience of the British Left from late 1920:

"As for these democrats whose eyes are fixed on the ends of the earth and who boast a soul far above trifles such as these, let them wear the labels fashioned for them by capitalist-imperialist England, for is this not a (nominally) free land and are not fools and their folly proverbially difficult to separate." (24)

One such folly was to win the debate after the 1922 Election - namely that socialism could be won in the House of Commons. The British superstition. The same

folly that Kessock hoped for in 1907. That was in the
future. MacLean's spiritual journey of discovery - so to
speak - from being Soviet Consul to thinking about
Scottish representation at Paris in 1918 to hailing a
Workers' Republic for all in 1920 included a physical
journey across the water to Ireland. He may have missed
out by not going to Russia in his lifetime but he
received a political and cultural education from real
revolutionaries who got the link between the national
and social questions far better than the Scots ever did.

THE TRAMP TRUST UNLIMITED.
Sandy Ross   Jas. D. MacDougall
Peter Marshall   John MacLean M.A.   Harry McShane

NOTES

(1)   Hugh MacDiarmid, *A Drunk Man looks at the Thistle*, 1987 edn, p.188

(2)   David Howell, *A Lost Left – Three Studies in Socialism and Nationalism*, 1986, p. 216

(3)   I'm a nationalist – just in case you didn't know!

(4)   Walter Kendall, *The Revolutionary Movement in Britain*, 1969, p.350

(5)   Tom Johnston, *Connolly and the Dublin Insurrection*, Forward, 6/5/16

(6)   Catholic Socialist Notes, Forward, 13/5/16.

(7)   Arthur McManus, *James Connolly: Socialist and Revolutionary*, the Socialist, 17/4/19.

(8)   Ian Mitchell, *A Bolshevik's visit to Lewis between the wars*, West Highland Free Press, 29/9/95.

(9)   Quoted in James D Young, *The Very Bastards of Creation: Scottish International Radicalism 1707 – 1995: A Biographical Study*, 1995, p.190

(10)   J O'Connor Kessack, *In Memory of the Stirling Martyrs*, Forward, 21/9/07

(11)   M Vajda, *The State and Socialism: Political Essays*, 1981, p. 91

(12)   Letters, *Forward*, 13/11/1915

(13)   The Scottish Review, Winter 1917, Back page advertisement

(14)   The Stornoway Gazette, 27/8/1920

(15)   James Hunter, *The Gaelic Connection: the Highlands, Ireland and nationalism, 1873-1922*, Scottish Historical Review, vol 54, 1975.

(16)   Ruaraidh Erskine, Guth na Bliadhna, 1918 , p. 101

(17)   Alasdair McCalluim, *Ruaraidh Arascainn is Mhairr*, Scottish Workers Republic, Spring 1997.

(18)   Erskine, *Cuisean Politiceach*, Guth na Bliadhna, An t-Samhraidh (Summer), 1921, p. 81. "There is a bitter struggle between town and country. The Marxists favour the urban dwellers but apart from a few followers of Marx who are

friends of the country, there is no real fondness among his disciples for rural issues."
Interestingly, MacLean had challenged Erskine to read Marx and Engels when approached about the Peace Conference. Ruaraidh rose to the challenge.

(19)   Erskine, Cuisean Politiceach, Guth na Bliadhna, An t-Earrach (Spring) 1921, p.5. Over the last while the country folk haves earched for their own bread and went hungry at the expense of the urban dwellers with their only recompense is the rattle and the bawling of Karl Marx. Well, Karl Marx is dead but the Celtic Gospel lives on.

(20)   Nan Milton, *John MacLean*, 1973, p.215-6.

(21)   *Scots National League: Great Protest Demonstration at Arbroath*, Liberty, October 1920.

(22)   For an excellent pen picture of Gillies see Stephen Coyle, *William Gillies - Portrait of a Patriot*, Scottish Workers Republic, Spring 1997.

(23)   Liam Mac Gille Iosa (Gillies), *How the Republic Went Down*, Liberty, November 1920

(24)   Erskine, *The British Superstition*, Liberty, October 1920

Chapter 7 - John MacLean - Green Clydesider

Hello Pat Malone, sure I knew you'd be here son

The red and the green we'll wear side by side.

- Hamish Henderson (1)

Two hundred thousand men - and what men! People who have
nothing to lose, two-thirds of whom are clothed in rags,
genuine proletarians and sans culottes and, moreover,
Irishmen, wild, headstrong, fanatical Gaels. One who has
never seen Irishmen cannot know them. Give me two
hundred thousand Irishmen and I will overthrow the
entire British monarchy.

- Frederick Engels (2)

The 1916 rising in Dublin passed MacLean by just as it
passed almost the whole British left by. He was doing
his second stint in jail for sedition. It is said that
those Irish republicans who were sentenced after the
Rising went to republican universities - mainly Frongoch
internment camp in Wales but other jails too - to study
and reflect and prepare for the next phase of the
struggle.

MacLean may have experienced some of this for himself in
Peterhead jail in 1918. This was his third stint in
prison after he had accused capitalism so powerfully
from the dock. He came out of prison and went into
election campaigning in the Gorbals. Yet it is his eve
of poll speech which is really interesting. He raised
the cause of Eugene Debs and big Bill Haywood who were
in American jails but he also called for the audience to
raise a protest for an imprisoned tax officer from
Lanark and two Sinn Fein prisoners who were still in
Peterhead - Barney Friel and Joe Robinson. This was
almost a throwaway line in Nan Milton's biography of her
father but it is rich in significance. (3) As we have
seen the Scotsman's account of his speech on release

from prison had an unnamed Sinn Feiner calling for a vote for MacLean as a friend of his Party.

How many Labour candidates in 1918 were calling for the release of Sinn Fein prisoners? Answers on a postcard please. And in line with what came after in MacLean's life it is not something that any of his biographers have pursued. MacLean must have been in contact and conversation with these guys. We can only surmise the way that the conversation would have went but it is worth reflection.

Joe Robinson - or Captain Joe Robinson - was a key player in Irish republican circles in Glasgow. He had joined the militant Boy Scout organisation, Na Fianna Èireann, in 1910 with his brother Seumas. He would soon become Commandant as well as being introduced into the secretive Irish Republican Brotherhood (IRB) in Glasgow. Along with the Scottish republican, Seumas Reader, he was making plans and running guns for the Scots Irish who would fight in the Easter Rising. This would result in around 60 volunteers from the West of Scotland based in the Kimmage Garrison in Dublin fighting for the Republic. (4) Joe Robinson was arrested in January and would not play any part in the rebellion.

By 1918 he was in jail again for theft - the theft of guns and ammunition that is! This is where he met the Red Clydesider. Robinson would become the Commandant of A Company and effectively the IRA in Scotland by 1920. Barney Friel was out in 1916 and was noted during the Rising for concocting a plan to disperse the looters - setting up buckets of cold water that would be triggered and fall on top of them so dispersing them as the previous tactic of firing over their heads didn't work. (5) The three men must have talked as they fraternised on the grounds of the prison in between making the famous brown post bags. MacLean must have listened intently as Robinson and Friel filled him in on the Irish situation: what happened in 1916, its significance, the true extent of Irish national feeling

and how it survived in the immigrant community in
Scotland.

Joe Robinson

Robinson must have been aware of the political situation
across Ireland as Sinn Fein prepared for the 1918
General Election on the back of Irish anger at the
executions of 16 leaders including Edinburgh's own James
Connolly and the homecoming of some of the prisoners
from their 'universities.' Indeed, Captain Joe was a
candidate himself for the North Down constituency.

Now this is surmising. Pure speculation which has no
place in a serious biography right? But I still can't

help thinking that why else would MacLean, the loyal BSP member, come out and call for the release of two Sinn Fein prisoners with such passion?

In an excellent article for the *History Ireland* magazine, Gavin Foster argues that John "was not initially sensitive to Irish nationalist aspirations." He argues that maybe some of his old Calvinist upbringing tinged his views on Irish Home Rule which meant that Ireland was looking at becoming a reactionary Catholic State without the class struggle. (6)

It is certainly true that MacLean had been in Ireland in 1907 and hadn't come back enthused about Irish nationalism. He had stayed in Belfast during the famous Dock Strike, with Jim Larkin from 6 - 9 August as a guest of the Socialist Society. He did produce accounts for readers across the water of the heroism of the strikers. He was there first hand to witness the Gordon Highlanders shooting at rioters on the Falls Road. He called the Government 'murderers' and provoked the ire of a future Labour Chancellor, Philip Snowden who called MacLean, "a fool of the most colossal dimensions." (7)

Those who beat the big lambeg drums and wear sashes did leave an impression for him as witnessed by his periodic referrals in his articles to the Orangemen generally and Sir Edward Carson in particular. MacLean saw through the Dublin born aristocrat and raised consciousness among the Left in Scotland as to the bigoted game he was playing. He remarked on, "the ignorance of Orangemen who lack the redeeming wit of the Irish Celt." (8) The occasion was a visit from Carson and his "deification" in the Press.

His contempt for Ulster Unionism was also demonstrated in his campaign to reinstate a teacher, Miss Marshall, dismissed by Dalziel School Board on the grounds that she had become a Catholic. That same school board were trying to push through a Protestant oath that should be taken by all teachers. MacLean objected on behalf of

Agnostic and Atheist teachers (his own distinction) and pointed his accusing finger in a political direction:

"Have they to be precluded from the teaching profession simply to suit the whims of, I am persuaded, Ulster bigots? Never! Scotland has not openly disgraced itself thus in its past history, though in rural areas Atheists and Agnostics have secretly had to suffer; so let us hope that not only teachers, but educationists, and especially working-class bodies, will see to it that the Dalziel Board, get no grant until the above obnoxious confession of faith is expunged from the teachers' agreement." (9)

It is fair to say that his sojourn in Belfast, friendship with Larkin and political observations had given him a view of Orange and Green on both sides of the water. Back then in the socialist army that was the BSP it was all about class. The Irish (or Scottish) national question did not compute to a British socialist when worker was fighting boss. It did compute to Irish socialists who were well in advance in the debates on the inter relationship between class and nationality.

At the General Election in 1918 it would come back to the fore. The people of the Gorbals were electing a Liberal in preference to MacLean. The people of Ireland were electing Sinn Fein MP's and rejecting the old Irish Party of Redmond and Dillon. A real national revolution was beginning in Ireland. 75 MP's including socialists such as Constance Markievicz (heroine of 1916 and the first ever woman elected to Parliament) and Liam Mellows. Many of those elected were still in prison.

While we in Scotland were debating our right to be represented at the Paris Peace conference the Irish had asserted that right at the ballot box - the very incarnation of President Woodrow Wilson's view that small nations should have self-determination. The Sinn Feiners asserted this right in the most peaceable yet revolutionary way. They abstained from Westminster and formed their own parliament. On the 21st January 1919 the

first Dáil Éireann or Irish Parliament assembled since
Grattan's parliament in the eighteenth century. A new
declaration of independence was read aloud by Cathal
Brugha and after it had also been read in French (the
language of diplomacy) by George Gavan Duffy, Brugha
said:

"Deputies, you understand from what is stated in this
Declaration that we have cut ourselves free from
England. Let the world know it and those who are
concerned bear it in mind. For come what may now,
whether it be death itself, the great deed is done."
(10)

The unravelling of events in Ireland would have a
massive impact on MacLean's political thought and
activities. His daughter, Nan, recalled that one of her
earliest childhood memories of the family home in
Auldhouse Road was a photo of the first Dáil in the
centre of the wall with de Valera in the middle of the
photo:

"I know my father was excited and encouraged by this
great event." (11)

The excitement and the encouragement would have been
picked up from Barney and Joe in Peterhead. It is only
recently, with the discovery of Seumas Reader's private
papers that we can truly gauge the level of MacLean's
excitement as he made political contact with Irish
republicans in the West of Scotland. In January 1919 John
MacLean arranged to meet some of the members of A Company,
Glasgow, Irish Republican Army, in Risk Street in the
Calton area of the East End. At this time A Company was
in close touch with the Irish Citizen Army in Dublin. At
that time, MacLean was the means of getting new sources
of munitions supplies from Scottish miners to 'A' Company
and later to the purchasing group under G.H.Q. Dublin.
Reader himself tells how the Risk Street meeting went:

"At the meeting in Risk Street, Glasgow, present were:
Alex Carmichael, F. Moran, Liam Gribbon, Me, Phil Graham

and P McCallum. The last three represented the Scottish Military Board of the I.R.B. and the former three were members of the I.R.B. who had left the organisation when Joe Robinson withdrew from the Glasgow Central Circle, but they had apologised after explanations from P. Carney and S. McGarry. We welcomed John MacLean who was accompanied by M. McGuire of 'A' Company. McGuire had already explained to MacLean that we would only be interested in matters of a military nature and not to be giving us a lecture on economics or political science." (12)

Mr McGuire clearly knew his guest's love of the dismal science. Now wasn't the time or place for politicking. They were talking about a revolution and how to practically support it. Seumas goes on:

"He got to the point by telling us that there was unrest in Scotland and, on no account should we bring the Irish War into Scotland as such because it would lead to sectarian hatred. He said that there should be co-ordination or federation with the Scots-Irish and the other revolutionary groups in Scotland, England and Wales. He was told that a G.H.Q. representative from Ireland would be here in Scotland to organise the purchase of arms and munitions, and the transport of same to Ireland. And as it had taken years to build our movement we were anxious that the job in hand should be a success and that he could be of invaluable assistance to the Irish cause, also, that from our observations and consultation, did not see any hope of an armed revolt on the Clyde.

MacLean admitted that very few of the Socialist Leaders believed in the use of arms, but that the Scottish ex-servicemen were coming to the fore, and that a Revolutionary plan had been drawn up with the intended formation of workshop committees, District Councils, National Councils, co-operative movement for the distribution of the necessities of life. According to John

Foster there were 2,000 demobbed and some were involved in drilling."

Seumas Reader's papers open up a whole new insight into John MacLean's thinking at this time and explain his evolution over the next couple of years. He was renowned as an opponent of war while the trenches blotted Europe's landscape but he was never a pacifist in that sense. It was the fact that workers were being encouraged to fight for two sets of capitalists. Now, the end of the war and the events in Russia put thoughts of revolution foremost in MacLean's mind. What is clear from these early discussions was the agenda that was forming: in MacLean's mind. He did not want Orange and Green battling out on the Clyde and he was looking at cooperation between the republicans and the revolutionary groups on his side of the water; for the Irish delegation there was only one cause and that was the cause of Ireland and nothing could or should deviate from this. The latter position would not waver while the former agenda – that of MacLean – would evolve greatly. Yet there is no doubting that the evolution in MacLean's thought, as he looked through the prism of Ireland, was well under way:

"MacLean reported the formation of District units of the Scottish Citizen Army, for discipline, City Street patrols, crofter patrols, Defence forces, the Black Brigade of Miners, Clyde Brigade of Engineers and Clyde workers."

There may have been exaggeration in the report of the actual formation of a Scottish Citizen Army at that time but there is no doubting that was the intention mirrored by the militant nationalists' attempt to form a Fianna ha h-Alba to mirror what was going on in Ireland. Stephen Coyle picks up the story:

"Before leaving the hall, John MacLean told Reader that not only would he show him notes, but that he would give him them, which concerned James Connolly and discussions regarding the formation of a Citizen Army in the year 1901 and 1909 by the Social Democratic Federation. Reader states he did not see or get these notes or papers, but A. McGill told him later that either James Maxton M.P. or Tom Bell got them when John MacLean died." (13)

A McGill was a left nationalist and contributor to Liberty. It is significant because there is not a peep about this in Tom Bell's biography and John Broom records how Maxton started and abandoned a biography of MacLean. Was it suppressed and politically buried? We will never know.

In May of that year Constance Markievicz, MacLean and John Wheatley spoke at the massive May Day rally in Glasgow attended by over 100,000 people including demobbed Russian sailors and many from the Irish community. Red flags and Irish tricolours flying side by side – Red and Green. The Soldiers Song was sung along with the Red Flag. The strong Irish presence on the rally mirrored activity taking place across Scotland. The Irish community was mobilising in support of the struggle back across the water. The number of Sinn Fein clubs in Scotland increased from 36 to 118 with tighter organisation from Sinn Fein itself. The Countess would have played her part by raising awareness of what was going on across the water to the wider left in Scotland. MacLean answered the call.

During her stay in Glasgow the Countess had consultations with John MacLean and promised him that she would contemplate on his suggestions on Irish and Scottish Defence Forces Federation. She was also to make a report to Irish Army Officials in Dublin.

When Seamus Reader approached Markievicz on what matters the two socialists had been discussing, she said that she was, "arranging for MacLean to visit Dublin and that the Irish in Scotland should work in some federal way with the most advanced Scottish organisations as she was aware that strong links existed."

The Countess, Markievicz addressing a crowd in Boston.

In June he went over to Dublin to attend a commemoration
of James Connolly's birthday. There is no hard evidence
that the two Marxists ever met each other. The late Jim
Young asserts that they never met. (14) Jim was
Secretary of the John MacLean Society in the 1990's. Its
Treasurer, John Ford, was adamant that they did as they
must have moved around similar Left circles. I am fond
of them both and there was always a good ding dong on
this one! MacLean used his speech to call for a Connolly
memorial workers college. (15) Interestingly no mention
is made at this stage of 'my pal, Jim.'

128

There is no doubting his admiration of Connolly whom he would describe a year later as, "the brain centre of the Irish working class." Connolly's influence did not die with him in 1916:

"His murder by the British government roused the latent fires in Irish breasts, and every subtle and unscrupulous move made by Ian McPherson and his minions at Dublin Castle but added to those fires, fires that never again will be quenched even by a general massacre until an Irish Republic has been established." (16)

His Irish education continued as he spent a month or so in Dublin surveying the scene as the phoney war continued between the British State and the Dáil. It is Dr Gavin Foster who truly brings out the extent of MacLean's political education. To read MacLean's account, under the heading 'Impressions of Dublin' from August 1919 there is a bit of self-justification going on. He refers to his speech in the Irish Workers Hall:

"There I urged that Ireland alone could never gain her own freedom, that her republic depended on the revolt and success of British labour, and that therefore Irish workers should not antagonise the soldiers of occupation in Ireland, but should try to win them over to the Irish point of view; further that Irish labour would not be free under a Sinn Fein republic, but only under a socialist workers republic…..They clearly comprehended the position I urged, and the ultimate advantage of it from the world workers' point of view." (17)

MacLean, like many men of the Left, could be quite egotistical. Not always quick to say 'I'm wrong.' But he was wrong. Ireland would still be waiting if they were waiting on British labour and the conversion of British troops. To be fair he did point out some "good natured correction" from his Irish hosts on the use of such terms as Home Rule and the Mainland. Foster takes this further calling MacLean's comments "indelicate" and pointing out that some of the response was hostile. (18) This was the true nature of MacLean's learning. The

importance of language and culture in the socialist
struggle. British socialists didn't get it. While he was
a British socialist he didn't fully get it either.

Before he got his Scottish education from left
nationalists in history and culture and identity, it was
Irish socialists who were paving the way for his
thoughts on Scotland. He could see just how important
the national struggle was to the Left in Ireland. He
witnessed a real anti-imperialism and he could see that
Britain was oppressing Ireland not just through class
but nationally too by denying Ireland her democratic
rights. He saw the army of occupation and by this stage
he was talking about 'Irish freedom.' What Foster calls
a "moral suasion" was taking place. He could and would
see that the Sinn Feiners were posing a greater threat
to the British State than British Bolsheviks. It was
also pointed out to him that there were Scottish
regiments in Ireland suppressing the population. What
was he doing about that as a Scottish socialist?

John got the boat back from Dublin with his head reeling
from these debates and discussions. How do you square
the language of national freedom with the international
cause of socialism; with defending the stand being made
by Russia.

In late 1919, as we have seen, he made his first
reference to a Scottish Communist Republic in a speech
in the Clyde Valley and compared a Labour vote with a
Sinn Fein vote in Ireland. He joined Marr's National
Committee and started thinking about his own country. As
he put it in 1920:

"Britain believes in self-determination for the races
under the heel of the late tsar but not for the races
under the sway of his kinsman, George 'Windsor'". (19)

MacLean may have upset his Irish hosts that summer but
he was to be right about one thing. Britain would
provoke a war with republican Ireland. The 1918 election
had been an overwhelming vote for Irish independence and

the meeting of the Dáil had been an act of rebellion in British eyes. Once the first shootings had been provoked, in poured the Army. As 1920 progressed the war became more brutal.

The Green Clyde mobilised. I first heard this term from my friend, Stephen Coyle during a talk to the John MacLean Society although Stephen does not lay claim to the term. Republicans in the West of Scotland along with other sympathisers from the Irish diaspora raised funds, organised meetings and ran guns over the water. (20) Even the Albion Rovers football ground in Coatbridge became a key venue for raising funds! MacLean too mobilised as did the nationalist left in Scotland.

In the summer of 1920 Maclean was addressing meetings and writing extensively on Ireland. In his Vanguard newspaper the Irish cause was declared and he dared his Scottish readers to take sides. With his Tramp Trust Unlimited (a collective of himself, Harry McShane, Sandy Ross, Peter Marshall and James McDougall) a massive 20,000 copies of his pamphlet, The Irish Tragedy: Scotland's Disgrace were sold across the central belt. The Disgrace he referred to was the use of Scottish troops in the British forces suppressing Ireland.   It is no accident that his Irish writings increased for MacLean went back to Dublin in the summer of 1920 and curiously did not write anything about this visit other than a mention (already noted) about making his way to Stornoway after returning from Dublin. MacLean had a revolutionary motive for returning to Ireland. During the Civil War in 1922 Seumas Reader has noted in his memoirs that an acquaintance of MacLean's ran guns over to Ireland:

"Saturday 1st July

John MacLean's agent Stuart McGregor was getting 7 pistols and ammunition aboard a boat for Dublin. I arranged to sail (in the same boat) sat night 1st July." (21)

If the best indicator of future performance is past
performance, then MacLean and his 'agents' were probably
doing something similar in the summer of 1920. As
Stephen Coyle has shown in his *High Noon on High Street*
there was similar activity among militant Scottish
nationalists. Hold the bus – wasn't MacLean fraternising
with some of those people? It really is fair to say that
in word and deed he supported the cause of Ireland.

Seamus Reader

Back in 1920 this was supported in Scotland by his
'fighting programme' which he called "Hands off
Ireland." Meetings were organised and 100,000 leaflets
distributed under the title, Proposed Irish Massacre!
This leaflet was puritan in so many ways talking about
proposed wars with America and calling for a general
strike of Scotland's workers to support Ireland. He was
urging Scots to 'Remember Bannockburn and Flodden. Read
again Burns' Scots Wha Hae.' John himself tells the
story of one such meeting or the 'battle of Motherwell'

as he called it in the Vanguard. Orangemen had come along to break up the meeting. MacLean decided to meet taunts with taunts in a reference to old Derry's walls:

"when I told the crowd that the Sinn Feiners and nationalists by vote in January had captured Derry and therefore Derry walls had surrendered, this galling statement was too much for the hooligans who had come to enrage me." (22)

John goes on to explain the scene of an old fashioned Orange and Green rammy with Orangemen charging shouting 'Up, Derry' and the nationalists in the meeting counter-attacking with shouts of 'Up, Dublin.' MacLean claimed this battle of Motherwell as a victory for the 'Sinn Fein Volunteers' claiming that it would give rise to new Volunteer companies in Scotland.

You may ask, from a political standpoint, what is the Marxist position on the Irish national question? The foremost Marxist in the British Isles answered this quite conclusively: we've got Derry's walls and you don't! Nah, nah, nah, nah nah! It is clear that over the summer of 1920 MacLean was talking a different lingo. His language grew more and more nationalist in tone. Language and culture intermingled. And this is what is most significant. MacLean finished his article with what would be his own battle cry over the remaining 3 years of his life:

"Up, Ireland! Up, Scotland! Up, the Social Revolution!"

On their own merits, MacLean performed sterling solidarity work for the Irish cause. But there is more to it. To read the Irish Tragedy pamphlet for the first time you may get lost in the analysis. Britain's motive in Ireland was to prevent the use of Irish ports by America in a future war with Britain. MacLean was wrong on this front although he based it in contemporary rumblings on both sides of the Atlantic. (23)

To read the pamphlet though in more detail is to be impressed with the level of factual information that MacLean had to hand. His section on the suppression of the republican press and Sinn Fein is to the exact date. His sub section on acts of aggression through 1919 and 1920 list the activities, the names of those killed or injured by the British army from Banbridge to Limerick; from Sligo to Dublin concluding:

"So I might continue itemizing the bloody butchery right down to the time of writing this pamphlet were I not sick of the whole murderous business." (24)

He had already informed readers in The Vanguard in June 1920:

"From May 1916 to December 1919 there have been 59 murders, 2084 deportations, 575 armed assaults on unarmed civilians, 14,153 raids on private homes, 5641 arrests, 2038 sentences, 56 suppressions of newspapers, 506 court martials…" (25)

There are more and more bits and pieces of a jigsaw that connect Mellows and the socialist wing of the IRB with MacLean. He couldn't have got this info from the British press or from the British left. This must have come from close contact with comrades connected to the struggle – Green Clydesiders as well as his visit to Ireland in the summer of 1920.

At this time MacLean was still working with the Scottish Labour College. He was still lecturing in Marxian economics and in philosophy. A member of his class for the academic year 1920 - 21 was Andrew Fagan, the Quartermaster of the Scottish Brigade of the IRA. He had come over to Scotland from County Meath and had entertained Constance Markievicz, Liam Mellows and Dan Breen. Stephen Coyle writes that Fagan was an outstanding pupil of MacLean's at the College. (26) It would appear that the education was two way. Fagan learned about philosophy and economics, MacLean learned about the Irish revolution.

Andrew Fagan would be a participant in the raid to free Frank Carty from a police van outside Duke Street prison in Glasgow in May 1921 - the 'high noon on High Street.' In the aftermath of this incident in which a policeman, Inspector Robert Johnston, was shot dead, a young priest named Father MacRory from St Mary's parish in the Calton was arrested with 19 other parishioners. To read MacLean's account in the Socialist is to read the words of someone in the know - a fellow Green Clydesider. (27) He reported on a raid on the offices of the Labour College and the suppression of socialist activists as well as those from the Irish community. He would urge caution that the Irish community should not react by premature action at a time when there was unrest in the mining communities and the State would come down heavy. He would soon feel this himself and be arrested again!

There is another interesting piece of the jigsaw. MacLean wrote in his election address in November 1922, when he stood as an independent Red candidate, that, "when Jim Connolly saw how things were going in Edinburgh he resolved on the Easter rebellion in Dublin." (28) The Edinburgh reference ia reference to his trial although this has usually been brushed aside as an outlandish claim. Yet Nan wrote in a magazine in 1979 stating that Seamus Reader wrote to her eleven years earlier:

"Your father was right in his remarks about James Connolly, because of anti-conscription and the intended revolt on the Clyde did influence Countess Markievicz, James Connolly and Sean MacDiarmid. They were determined that at least the Liffey would assert itself."

Nan goes on:

"Reader also told me that MacLean had association with the Irish Republican Movement in Scotland, that he often carried reports to Dublin concerning him and that 'after the 1916 rising and his release from prison he had contacts with some members of the Scottish Divisional Board of the Irish Republican Brotherhood.'" (29)

Reader was also a Scottish republican as well as a gun
runner from the Green Clyde. He was there and his
account is backed up in a recent biography of the first
President, Patrick Pearse:

"Reader briefed Connolly on Scotland when they met in
the Connolly lodgings at the Markievicz home on Leinster
Road on 17 January 1916. Connolly was upbeat about the
prospect of receiving armaments from unionised
dockworkers, seamen and cattle drovers on the Glasgow –
Dublin route." (30)

It falls into place that the Red Clyde may have assisted
Ireland's opportunity in 1916 but it was the Green Clyde
that definitely mobilised. It all fell into place for
John MacLean when he fraternised with Joe Robinson and
Barney Friel in 1918 in Peterhead. I am absolutely
convinced of this.

MacLean's experience drew him into direct support for
the Irish cause. In Ireland he saw the British Empire or
John Bull in action. In 1914 he opposed the First world
war and condemned all imperialism from an
internationalist standpoint but he did not understand
the true nature of the UK. By November 1920 his critique
of British imperialism led him to ask the question:

"I hold that the British empire is the greatest menace
to the human race. Lloyd George's Caernarvon speech
proves it. The best interests of humanity can therefore
be served by the break-up of the British empire. The
Irish, the Indians and others are playing their part.
Why ought not the Scottish?" (31)

Now Scotland was not Ireland but the question was
pertinent as the national question hadn't/hasn't gone
away in Scotland and the debate was going on within the
left. Why ought not the Scottish? Erskine of Marr and
Gillies were also pitching in with solidarity work.
Erskine's group had been inspired by the electoral rise
of Sinn Féin. They were inspired by their very name. In
Guth na Bliadhna in the Winter of 1918 Erskine wrote:

" Chaidh fhaighnich dhinn a cheann ghoirid an caomh leinn 'Sinn Féin', a phrionsapalan agus a chuid mhodhannan?..... Is caomh leinn da rireabh 'Sinn Féin' agus na prionsapalan agus a mhodhannan a ta e a' cur an cleachdadh ann an Eirinn, ta iad sin a' lionadh ar suila mar nach b'olc." (32)

Their articles in Liberty mirrored many of the articles in the Vanguard in 1920.

The most poignant was the article on the Funeral of Terence MacSwiney, the martyred Lord Mayor of Cork in November 1920 who had died on hunger strike in prison. A deputation from the Scots National League had attended the funeral. They had placed a wreath with the card:

"Sith an dèigh stri

Buaidh tre bhais

Beir gradh is urram

Bhon Ghàidheal na h-Albann." (33)

The solidarity is significant despite the comparative weakness of Scottish nationalism. As I write, in 2017, many Scottish nationalists still don't want to talk about Ireland. It is a political hot potato. Back then, in the days before the SNP existed, nationalists in Scotland were rallying in support of their fellow Gaels. The pages of Liberty in 1920 were full of reports and commentary on the war of independence. (34) Like MacLean, the magazine exposed the barbarities of British rule and called for Scottish solidarity. MacLean also used the opportunity of MacSwiney's death:

"Comrades, champion Ireland's cause with trebled energy and thus avenge the martyred Lord Mayor. Never in all our reading of history have we read of a slower and more cruel torture than that practiced in Brixton prison." (35)

We cannot underestimate the role that John MacLean played as a 'champion' of Ireland's cause. In the MacLean papers in the National Library of Scotland in Edinburgh there is a postcard that was sent to MacLean in late 1922. It is a James Connolly postcard with an image of an Irish Citizen Army soldier and of the Fianna and was sent to MacLean by Robert de Coeur, himself a member of the Citizen Army and who had fought at St Stephens Green in the 1916 rising and in the war of independence. (36) The postcard congratulates MacLean on his release from prison (his fifth and last term) with a prayer to God to strengthen him. In a reference to Connolly, de Coeur wrote:

"..that day for which I fought for him may soon dawn, a free Ireland inside the Internationale." (37)

Thanks to the papers of Seumas Reader we get to know how much of a Green Clydesider MacLean actually was and the full extent of his solidarity work for Ireland and de Coeur's postcard is just one example of how much he was known and appreciated in Ireland for his activity. Also there is the evidence of C Desmond Greaves who wrote:

"During the revolutionary period of 1919 -21, of all the leaders, John MacLean seems most strongly of the view that the Scottish workers themselves must pass from words to deeds." (38)

MacLean was keen that Scotland in general and the Scottish working class in particular should be on Ireland's side. He brushed aside the partitionist claims of the Ulster unionists whose arguments would have been seductive to a Scottish Protestant constituency:

"Do not be deceived by the Ulster argument which is as much of a lie as the 'defence of Belgium' excuse for entering into the late War." (39)

Gavin Foster summarises:

"Whatever about his place in the history of European socialism or Scottish nationalism, his passionate engagement with Ireland's struggle for independence - in particular his insistence on its imperial context and potential global significance - deserves consideration in any thorough examination of the Irish Revolution." (40)

This passionate engagement continued up until his death. Dr Foster unearthed a letter from MacLean to 'President Cosgrove' in November 1922 protesting against the execution of republican prisoners during the Civil War in Ireland. This letter was also printed in full in the *Socialist* in December 1922. He addressed himself on behalf of, " four thousand 'Red' and 'Green' supporters of a Scottish Workers Republic." (41) He expressed his "dismay and disgust" while illustrating that he understood the situation:

"No Scotsman appreciates more than I do the tight corner into which John Bull has placed the Irish 'Free' State."

That said MacLean could not understand why Irish republicans should be executed by their former comrades. His letter was prompted from motions passed at a meeting in the St Mungo's Hall. Along with the other Scottish solidarity we have witnessed MacLean felt that he could link the causes:

"We trust for the sake of Irish and Scottish Republicanism no other executions will take place…"

MacLean made special reference to the case of Erskine Childers who was awaiting execution. Childers was a writer of English descent and had been one of the Irish negotiators at the peace talks in London with Collins and Arthur Griffith. He opposed the proposed Treaty and came out for the republican side in the Civil War and paid the ultimate price. It is fitting that MacLean made this plea - futile though it may have been - as Childers showed some Irish internationalism before his execution:

"I die full of love for Ireland. I die loving England and praying that she will change completely and finally towards Ireland." (42)

Erskine Childers

This brave man expressed his soon to be unnatural and enforced death, way before his time, as beautifully and bravely as anyone:

"It is 6 a.m. – it all seems simple and inevitable like lying down after a long day's work."

The Scottish sympathiser's long day's work would continue for a wee while yet and his political journey was expressed in his sign off to the letter. "Yours for an Irish Republic, John MacLean." (43) Not socialist,

not workers just Irish. He hadn't abandoned the cause of
the Socialist Republic or his hope that Jim Larkin
should be the first Communist President of Ireland; he
just prioritised that's all.

Red and Green again.

This mingling of Red and Green led him back to Dublin in
the summer of 1923 to meet James Larkin. It was a kind
of political holiday. By his own admission, he headed
straight for Liberty Hall obviously on some errand and
had all his expenses paid for him. He related this in a
letter to his daughters dated 3rd July. He went over with
"two friends." Peter Marshall and James Hamilton and it
was the latter who paid for the trip. What is
interesting is that in this letter he calls Connolly, "a
friend of mine" - so did they meet? - and relays the
events of 1916 in nationalist language:

"After Connolly was wounded he surrendered. The dirty
English government had him shot along with other brave
Irishmen."

He saw first-hand the devastation caused by the Civil
War following the Treaty and in his mini-historical
analysis for his daughters he blamed the English for
setting comrade against comrade.

His mingling of red and green also led him to welcome
the Countess to Glasgow who spoke three times for him at
the hustings as he took his Scottish Workers Republic to
the ballot box in late 1922 and 1923 before his death.

Ireland was a prism for MacLean. It was through the
prism of Ireland that he re-examined his views on the
nature of imperialism, his thoughts about his own
country and his roots in the Gàidhealtachd. It was
through the prism of Ireland that he came to call
himself a Scottish Republican and would lead to his
break with British socialism. Just as he had learned
from left leaning nationalists in his own country so too
did he learn from Irish socialists that you could be

part of the great Internationale without being part of a
not so great Union and Empire. MacLean summed this up
in his Vanguard newspaper:

"The Irish situation, obviously, is the most
revolutionary that has ever arisen in British history
but unfortunately lads who fancy themselves the only
revolutionaries are too stupid or too obsessed with some
little crotchet to see with sufficient clarity the tight
corner the Irish are placing Britain in." (44)

It was a swipe at the British Left that would explain
the other major political struggle of MacLean's post war
life. You see the 'lads' that he referred to were trying
to form a Communist Party…..of Great Britain.

NOTES

(1)   Hamish Henderson, The John MacLean March, 1948. This famous song was famously written for a meeting of the Scotland - USSR Friendship Society to commemorate the 25th anniversary of MacLean's death. I had the privilege of hearing Hamish sing it at a Great John MacLean Night in the Arches, Glasgow in 1998.

(2)   Frederick Engels, Letters from London, 27/6/1843, in *Marx - Engels, Ireland and the Irish Question*, 1986, p.35

(3)   Nan Milton, *John MacLean*, 1973, p. 182-3.

(4)   Martainn S Ó' Catháin, Irish Republicanism in Scotland 1858 - 1916: Fenians in Exile, 2007, p.239

(5)   Max Caulfield, *The Easter Rebellion*, 1916, ch.17. Friel and another prisoner, Michael O'Callaghan, went on hunger strike over their treatment as common criminals with no political status. I am indebted to Stephen Coyle for this information.

(6)   Gavin Foster, *Scotsmen, Stand by Ireland: John MacLean and the Irish Revolution*, History Ireland, Jan/Feb, 2008

(7)   John Gray, *City in Revolt: James Larkin and the Belfast Dock Strike of 1907*, 1985, p.167

(8)   Gael, Justice, 21/6/1913, p.6

(9)   Gael, Justice, 26/4/1913, p.6

(10)   David Hogan, *The Four Glorious Years*, 1953, p61.

(11)   Milton, ibid, p. 196

(12)   I am indebted to Eddi Reader, singer and great niece of Seumus for the quotes/references to her great uncle's memoirs and to Stephen Coyle for access to notes from a speech he gave to the John MacLean commemoration 26th November 2012.

(13)   Stephen Coyle, ibid.

(14)   John MacLean, The Irish Fight for Freedom, The Vanguard, June 1920

(15)   This comes across in a couple of Young's
writings on MacLean including his biography.

(16)   John MacLean, In the Rapids of Revolution,
1978, p.160

(17)   MacLean, ibid, p161-2

(18)   Foster, ibid

(19)   John MacLean, *The Irish Fight for Freedom*,
Vanguard, June 1920.

(20)   For a good account of this see John Burrowes,
Irish: The Remarkable saga of a City and a Nation,
2004 especially the chapter on the Glasgow
Shinners. I am also indebted to John Ford for some
invaluable information.

(21)   MacLean would have been still in Barlinnie
jail when Mr McGregor made his journey.

(22)   MacLean, *The Battle for Motherwell* and also
in Milton, ibid, p.239

(23)   See Graham Bain's pamphlet, *John MacLean –
His Life and Work, 1919 – 1923* for some
contemporary references. Also it is worth noting
that Eamon de Valera had to address "legitimate"
British fears that an independent Ireland would be
used by Britain's enemies to attack her when he
was in America raising funds and awareness for
Ireland's cause over 1920. See Hogan, *The Four
Glorious Years*, 1953, p. 258.

(24)   John MacLean, MA, *The Irish Tragedy:
Scotland's Disgrace*, John MacLean Society edition,
p.8

(25)   MacLean, *The Irish for Freedom*, The Vanguard,
June 1920

(26)   Stephen Coyle, *High Noon on High Street*,
2008, p.155

(27)   MacLean, *In the Rapids of Revolution*, p. 229.
His article was entitled *Scottish history in the
making.*

(28)   MacLean, ibid p.234

(29)   Milton, *John MacLean and Ireland*, Socialist
Scotland/Alba Soisealach, Winter/Geamhradh, 1979,
p.8-9

(30)   Ruán O'Donnell, *16 Lives - Patrick Pearse*, 2016, p131 - 132

(31)   MacLean, ibid, p.220

(32)   R Erskine of Mar, Guth na Bliadhna, An Geamradh, 1918, p. 416. "We asked ourselves recently do we like Sinn Féin, its principles and its methods? … We very much like Sinn Féin and their principles and its methods as they apply them in Ireland against those who commit evil in front of our eyes."

(33)   *Scots follow MacSwiney*, Liberty, November, 1920. The card translates - Peace after struggle, victory through death, with love and respect from the Scottish Gael.

(34)   For example, A McGill, MA, *The Case for Ireland*, Liberty, June 1920.

(35)   John MacLean, *Scotsmen Stand by Ireland*, The Vanguard, July 1920.

(36)   RM Fox, The History of the Irish Citizen Army, 1944, Appendix

(37)   John MacLean papers, NLS, Acc 4251

(38)   C Desmond Greaves, *Scotland and the Struggle for Irish Freedom*, Scot Marx, p.23

(39)   MacLean, *Scotsmen, Stand by Ireland!* The Vanguard, July 1920

(40)   Foster, ibid, p. 37

(41)   Foster, ibid, p. 37. Also the John MacLean supplement, *The Socialist*, December 1922

(42)   Quoted in Frances M Blake, The Irish Civil War, 1922-23. And what it still means for the Irish People, (West London United Troops Out Movement pamphlet) p. 22.

(43)   MacLean, *The* Socialist, December 1922

(44)   MacLean, ibid, p. 178 from *Up, India!* The Vanguard, August 1920.

Chapter 8 - The Party - Right or Wrong

There was a man and his name was Joe (oh Joe, good old Joe)

He had friends and they loved him so (oh good old Joe)

His friends all praised him to the sky (oh Joe, good old Joe)

But the good old soul he had to die (oh good old Joe)

When he died they had a wake (oh Joe, good old Joe)

His friends all found they'd made a mistake (oh poor old Joe) ….

When he got to Satan's feet (oh Joe, poor old Joe)

Nick got up and gave him his seat (oh poor old Joe.)

   - Matt McGinn (1)

Ever since John met Karl there was only one 'ism' for him and it defined him. Whatever guise Marxism took John MacLean usually fell in line. At one time it made you a Social Democrat; a bit later a Socialist in the BSP. The Bolshevik revolution in Russia saw the resurrection of the word 'communist.' After all the famous German with the big beard had co-wrote the **Communist Manifesto** in 1848 at a time of revolution in Europe.

Communism was not the preserve of Marx or Engels. In many ways it was a utopian idea summed up by the French philosopher, Saint-Simon who summed it up in a great call which Marx himself used; **from each according to ability, to each according to need.** So simple and so powerful. Was this not the philosophy of Jesus's 12 as they came to terms with life without him in the flesh? Was this not the ethos behind Thomas More's **Utopia**? Or what of the Anabaptists or Diggers in the seventeenth century? Communism had previous. Marx either made it

scientific or toxic depending on your point of view. He
challenged in 1848 religion, nation and property.

In 1919 the Bolsheviks' centralising tendency led them
toward one Party - the Communist Party and their
international organisation became the Communist
International or Comintern for short. John MacLean
lapped this up. If that was where the revolution was
going, then he would follow.

And yet it is a historical fact that a Communist Party
was formed in Britain without John MacLean. Why would
the foremost Marxist in the British Isles and the
appointed Soviet consul refuse to join? After all there
was a street named after him in St Petersburg - Prospect
Maklina and he was the honorary president of both the
Russian and short lived Hungarian soviet republics.
Surely Lenin would just have sent a communique saying,
"get a grip". There is a tale to tell and it is a
fascinating part of MacLean's life after 1918 and still
provokes debate among the Left.

In August 1920 there was a unity conference held in
Leeds to form one Party. Revolutionary unrest swept
through Europe and Asia with the end of World War One.
This manifested itself in class unrest, socialist
revolutions and anti-imperialist struggles. Germany,
Hungary, India and Ireland were hotspots. In Glasgow in
January 1919 the red flag was raised in George Square,
the forty hours' strike was called and the British
government responded by confining local troops to
Maryhill Barracks and sending 10,000 troops (mainly from
England) to the city. MacLean was on a speaking tour of
England and missed these tumultuous events.

So in August 1920 the main groupings came together - the
Labour Party excepted - to discuss the formation of one
Party. The British Socialist Party was the biggest
grouping and they took the lead in the negotiations. The
Bolsheviks in Russia knew their preferred outcome. This
same month John put out his "All Hail" leaflet.

By this time MacLean had been secretly expelled from the BSP. This had happened at the Easter 1920 conference. He had knocked too many noses out of joint with his criticisms of the Hands Off Russia campaign and its new recruit, the former Liberal Colonel Malone. Things came to a head when MacLean refused to share a platform with Malone on the grounds that Malone had been in the Reconstruction Committee which had worked to bring down the Revolution in Russia. In addition, John distrusted Theodore Rothstein (the Bolsheviks main conduit in Britain and who had also worked in the War Office as an interpreter.) The BSP was coming under increasing Russian financial dominance.

After refusing to share a platform MacLean's rebelliousness had made him a marked man. His suspicions were aroused when he was offered a full time role in the Hands off Russia campaigning group. He rejected. Revolutionary work at home would help Russia not meetings. MacLean suspected the British State at work. (2) The BSP themselves got to work. At the unity conference in August the Glasgow Tradeston Branch was not recognised as an affiliate. Guess who was a member of the Tradeston Branch?

Earlier in the year John's old Paisley buddie, Willie Gallacher, had gone to Russia. At the second congress of the Comintern he had heard Zinoviev say:

"The Communist Party must be strictly centralised, with an iron discipline, with a military organisation…In England we have four or five separate communist groups…This must be stopped." (3)

Gallacher had travelled to Russia illegally. He was told to get maximum unity and get the dissidents like MacLean on board. MacLean never made it to Russia. He refused to travel illegally and applied unsuccessfully on a couple of occasions for a visa to the Foreign Office. In his view of the world, he was still the Soviet Consul in Scotland and had every right to travel. It is certainly one of the fascinating 'what ifs' of left wing political history. What if MacLean had gone to Russia? Tom Bell, who would become one of the leaders of the new Party, wrote:

"It is a thousand pities that John MacLean never visited Soviet Russia…to see what he had been working for all his life." (4)

It is a seductive argument put across by a leading Communist to add some sprinkles on the view that MacLean chose isolation tactically, practically and politically. The truth reads a little bit different. The London based researcher, Jim Clayson, unearthed a wealth of material in the Home Office files. (5) Jim tells of MacLean's re-application on 17th June 1920 which was dealt with by an official named R H Hoare. There was no reason that Hoare could see why 'respectable persons' could not enter border states including, "politicians." So, Jim muses, there were no grounds to deny John a passport. What follows is simply dynamite. Back to Mr Hoare, civil servant:

"When the Socialist Party originally applied to send their deputation, I had an interview with them, and they mentioned MacLaine as one of the men they would probably send if permission was granted. I probably looked surprised at the mention of this name because a hasty explanation followed that he was not John MacLean, who is now applying for a passport but the other one and that they knew quite well that MacLean of Glasgow was mad."

As we will see this was part of a wider political campaign against MacLean that took the debate out of politics and into mental health. It had a major impact on John's passport application. Clayson picks this up:

"…there are members of the 'Socialist Party' who were keen to portray MacLean as 'mad.' Who were they??????"

What Jim's research shows is that in truth, it is a thousand pities that fellow socialists stopped John from going to Russia. They always were good at re-writing history in the Communist Party even before Comrade Joe succeeded Lenin.

Zinoviev's words show that the Bolsheviks did not appreciate the national question within Britain. Gallacher and co did not exactly enlighten them. The Scottish Question in particular would have seriously undermined the unity project and it was a real threat. MacLean was writing more and speaking more on Scottish issues and raised the alternative banner of a separate Scottish Communist Party. This was a real threat. Gallacher concedes in his *Revolt on the Clyde* that when the proposals for a united British party were being mooted the idea of a Scottish party was, "rapidly gaining ground" among the shop stewards and the group around MacLean. (6)

A thoroughly researched thesis on Rothstein's influence on the British labour movement by David Burke traces the roots of this Scottish autonomy back to the unrest around the time of the Easter 1916 BSP conference. The fall out between the London leadership of the Party under Hyndman and the Scottish group who supported the Zimmerwald conference was exacerbated by the Irish sections within the Scottish labour movement who rightly criticised the Party's silence on the Rising in Dublin. These events provoked a response from Rothstein writing under a pseudonym in *The Call*. Burke explains that the Russian delegate:

"…denied both the feasibility and desirability of small nation states within the global economy in accordance with the principles outlined at the second Zimmerwald conference. In Scotland accusations now began to appear accusing The Call, the BSP leadership and the Glasgow District Council of the BSP with cynically undermining attempts to develop a mass movement to demand Maclean's release, which had taken on a nationalist character." (7)

Burke's comments are revealing as they back up the tensions that MacLean felt at the political and organisational level. His thesis is not sympathetic to MacLean's hostility to join the Communist Party so it is an objective comment. Even after Hyndman left, the BSP leadership did little to campaign for MacLean's release from Peterhead to the point of actually undermining real attempts to secure his release. Equally significant is the British unionist line taken on the national questions in the British Isles with these comments coming from a Bolshevik who was supposed to stand for national autonomy for the peoples of the Old Russian Empire. Ideological cartwheels were being performed back in 1916-17 and the man in Peterhead wasn't really used to these type of cartwheels. He would ask himself what was the right thing to do.

MacLean still acted and felt this way in 1920 and the Party apparatchiks were concerned. In May MacLean had resurrected the Vanguard newspaper and soon formed the Tramp Trust Unlimited as a formidable campaigning group. He still did not like the BSP leadership – "the London gang" and doubted their honesty. This was backed up by a fellow traveller and friend, Sylvia Pankhurst who had a similar experience with Rothstein whom she accused of manipulating the unity vote by offering money from the International if they agreed with Lenin's position. (8)

MacLean had a motive and an alternative that was not off the wall but was consistent with his Marxism and the political debate in Scotland at that time. As we have seen he articulated this in August by his reference to the "Bolshevik notion of world communism through national communism." It was a clear break with the British Left and he would put it in a way that the CPGB could never condone let alone understand:

"Scotland is firmer for Marxism than any other part of the British Empire. Clyde speakers get bigger and better audiences in Scotland than speakers across the borders with very, very few exceptions. In other words Scotland is becoming more self-reliant than ever before and looks hopefully for a lead from men reared and trained on this side of the border." (9)

The CPGB could never condone this because they wanted to contest elections and send their elected members to the Imperial Parliament with Lenin's blessing. It therefore became internationalist to think in all-Britain terms and this view became the Labour party view in the 1930's too. To think in Scottish terms was 'parochial' and nationalist and it became easy to denounce 'claymore communists.' In a wider sense the CP leadership could not understand from their Third International viewpoint that MacLean was calling for an indigenous socialism rooted in time and place for his own country. The centralising tendencies of the Leninists who talked a good game about self-determination for oppressed peoples but were quick to base their socialism in the old imperial territories - Russia, GB, Spain, France - just as Rothstein had argued for back in 1916. If you don't believe me check their record on actually de-centralising into nationally self-determining units. Ask the Catalans, the Basques, the Baltic countries, the Corsicans and many more. The Irish got it and kept their autonomy as separate Left organisations and MacLean loved them for it.

MacLean, therefore, had to break with British socialism to advance his cause. In the CPGB internationalism and British unity meant the same thing and it is worth pointing out that the early CPGB did not cover themselves in glory on anti-imperialist issues. For instance, Tom Quelch told Lenin at the Second Congress of the Comintern that he could not ask English workers to support colonial uprisings. (10) Time and space prevents me from going into the theory that the British Empire could facilitate an easier transition to international socialism due to its inherently internationalist nature!

MacLean called for a Scottish Communist Party as
Scotland was a definite country under article 17 of the
Comintern's constitution. Bell in his biography concedes
this as "true enough." (11) Further, if England was to
be led by Malone and Rothstein then the Scots should
have their own organisation. Kendall develops this
point:

"MacLean had severe doubts about the independence and
integrity of the CPGB, marked misgivings regarding
certain of its leaders and was himself unwilling to
abide by Comintern directives until such time as its
leaders were better informed about the British
situation." (12)

Battle commenced for the heart and soul of communism in
Scotland and John took on the young Communist Party
machine. Long before uncle Joe Stalin the new
revolutionary party was developing some of the tricks
and techniques that would be associated with that tyrant
with the big moustache. In September 1920 a conference
was called in Glasgow to form a Scottish Communist
Labour Party and in the chair was John MacLean from
Glasgow. You would be forgiven for thinking that
MacLean's camp were organising their Scottish party but
it was all a ruse. It was a different MacLean (a unity
supporter) and it was to lure activists in to the fold.
Up popped a certain Willie Gallacher who spoke at the
conference for unity talks with the new British party.
How could you refuse?

For me this indicates two things. Firstly, that the
situation in Scotland must have been touch and go and
that the Communist leadership feared MacLean's
influence. This conference gave the illusion of creating
a Scottish party - which many activists favoured - while
its intention was to kill a separate party stone dead.
Clever eh? And all very Stalinist except that he wasn't
in power at that point. Secondly, when many on the Left
talk about retreat and isolation (13) it is important to

remember that MacLean did not choose isolation. A nascent political machine marginalised him.

No fair debate took place. The CP leadership hoodwinked many Scottish activists into joining the British Party with seductive arguments for socialist unity in the one Party. It wasn't all seduction though. MacLean's meetings were heckled and broken up by Gallacher's supporters. At this point MacLean found allies in Sylvia Pankhurst and in the Socialist Labour Party. MacLean called a meeting on Christmas day 1920 in the SLP rooms in Glasgow. Barbara Winslow's account is quite revealing:

"The CPGB was afraid not only of ideas but also of other socialists who were not ready or willing to join. Gallacher, now a leading CP functionary embarked on a campaign to wreck the left wing SLP. He and some political allies gatecrashed an SLP meeting organised by John Maclean in Glasgow on Christmas Day 1920. He repeatedly heckled the speakers and it seemed that the meeting would end in a fight. Violence was avoided but it seemed the Gallacher group continued heckling." (14)

Tom Bell was obviously among this group with Gallacher but he painted a different picture. In his biography of MacLean he stated that there was, "no appreciation of the national need as understood by MacLean." The SLP had most of their ties in England and were, in the CP's favourite jibe, 'sectarian.' John was "completely isolated." (15) You pays your money you takes your choice but I know who I believe.

About this same time Sylvia Pankhurst had come out of prison to be told that she had to hand over the ownership of her newspaper, the Workers Dreadnought, to the Party and that she should do this, "as a disciplined member of the Party." Sylvia called this a "political measles" that feared free expression. (16) Like MacLean she faced the full force of Gallacher's invective for not toeing the line as well as also facing the wrath of Saint Vladimir Lenin himself for daring to criticise the right wing nature of the BSP leadership. (17) What really strikes me is that this occurred in the heyday of a new Party that should be enwrapped in the fresh fervour of creative expression. Instead it is rigid orthodoxy and control and the crushing of dissent.

It certainly puts paid Bell's "thousand pities" theory as Sylvia did go to Russia, did join the Party and was banging her head against the proverbial brick wall. It would have made no difference at all had MacLean gone to Moscow. (18) She was duly expelled and she reminds the Left in the most beautiful way of the moral of the story;

"I shall never adopt the motto, 'The Party Right or Wrong' - I shall always go for what I believe to be best. I think that is the only way to avoid becoming a hindrance to progress. A Communist Party, a Party of Revolution, must, I think be very stern, very unyielding, very exclusive towards the Right elements, but ever tolerant towards the Left elements." (19)

Hindsight is easy isn't it? Neither MacLean nor Pankhurst had this luxury nor were they prescient. They could never have foreseen the real horrors of communism as they unfolded. They were communists who believed that it was the revolutionary force that would liberate not just the working class but humanity. They were zealots in that sense whose principles were overarching. What they could see, however, was increasing Moscow domination of the Comintern and they could see the British CP'ers, in Kendall's words, as puppets strutting on a Comintern stage.

MacLean articulated this concern in his Vanguard newspaper in December 1920 when he called for a Scottish Communist Party and made his invitation for all 'clear headed and honest' revolutionaries to come together in one camp (this would be the Christmas day meeting in the SLP rooms.) In a point which the British Left could not (and still don't) get MacLean argued:

"We in Scotland must not play second fiddle to any
organisation with headquarters in London, no more than
we would ask Dublin to bend to the will of London." (20)

Sylvia Pankhurst

And this included a sideswipe at Gallacher who was
'going the rounds ridiculing the idea' of a separate
Scottish Party, "because he has been to Russia and poses
as the gramophone of Lenin." More significantly he was
calling for autonomy in the British Isles:

"We stand for the Marxian method applied to British conditions. The less Russians interfere in the internal affairs of other countries at this juncture the better for the cause of revolution in those countries." (21)

It wasn't just MacLean. His comrades in the Socialist Labour Party were saying the same thing but from the Syndicalist point of view. This was put quite clearly in an article on Moscow and the SLP in March 1923:

"The man who would base his tactics in America, England or France on Russian experience must be innocent alike of history, economics and geography." (22)

The author of this article, John Henderson, wisely called for "a time for study" in the Left in the wake of the defeat of the various revolutions and the growth of fascism.

For his part, MacLean followed up his own critique with an Open Letter to Lenin in January 1921 though it is doubtful if the Russian leader ever saw it. It was published in the SLP's paper, *The Socialist*. This was significant as the SLP were fellow dissidents and also because the conference that would form the CPGB were meeting in Leeds on the day he published his letter. I have read this letter many times over the years and behind all the politicking and positioning and bluster lies a real hurt. He knew the British government were up to something and he knew that certain 'comrades' were up to something. He knew he was being marginalised and felt powerless to do anything about it.

He revealed that Gallacher was doing more than just bad mouthing the idea of a Scottish CP:

"He has been going round the country and warning socialists that MacLean is suffering from "hallucinations." He wrote to that effect to the SLP when I was arranging a conference to bring my supporters in line with the SLP and he squirmed when I read his letter in public." (23)

This really was low from Gallacher and as we shall see formed the basis of an on-going Communist Party narrative about him. John had been through a lot. Agnes had left him in the autumn of 1919. She probably couldn't take any more of the 'all for the cause' line and could see that he was physically and mentally exhausted. Agnes continued to stay in Glasgow for a spell with the girls staying with Aunts while she worked shifts. Young Nan took ill with pneumonia which took a lot of nursing from Mum who blamed the polluted Glasgow air and the female MacLeans left for Hawick.

It is true that he was exhausted and had been in jail three times. His papers in the National Library show letters from figures on the Left arguing that he needed to convalesce and MacLean had no intentions of doing this at such a revolutionary time in Europe's history. Like most men of the Left he perhaps didn't have the emotional intelligence to see where his wife was coming from. Agnes and the girls left and John went on to Lancashire, Ireland, the Western Isles. Just what his body needed eh?

This, however, didn't make him mad or hallucinatory. He was going through a difficult emotional time and his enemies were pressing bad emotional buttons. He reacted emotionally and I think you probably would too. In characteristic fashion he told Lenin:

"I am still carrying on, although betrayed, not by the workers but by so called 'comrades.'" (24)

Burke echoes Jim Clayson's point about the unholy alliance between the BSP leadership and the Home Office papers on MacLean's mental state. By 1920 the British Government felt that MacLean was "insane." While his old comrades may have used different language ("hallucinatory") its effect was the same. The Home Office could report with glee in late 1920 that Lenin had been informed by the Executive of the BSP of MacLean's "mental state" and that the Soviet Government had cut off relations even though he was still

officially Soviet Consul. (24) Again this must have cut
through John MacLean like a knife to the heart. He never
received any official communication from Moscow
rescinding his position. The Soviet Consul for Scotland
must have been one of the first non-persons as he was
written out of history by Lenin and his British
supporters.

He was hurt, he felt wronged but this wasn't the first
time he had been isolated and had stayed true to his
principles. He was keeping up the good fight. In a
reference to his work with the unemployed he mentioned
that 3,500 meet twice a week in Glasgow's city hall
discussing "principles and tactics." MacLean knew that
many were near starvation due to unemployment and he
reminded Lenin of the role that the Green Clydesiders
would play.

This is highly significant because John MacLean out of
the Communist Party was just as much of a threat to the
State. His Tramp Trust were organising the unemployed
into a Movement that the CP would learn from and take
over. It is no accident that the National Unemployed
Workers Movement was taken over by the CP at a time when
Harry McShane left the Tramp Trust to join the CPGB
himself. McShane himself maintains that the first
meeting of the unemployed was organised by the two of
them in November 1920 on Glasgow Green. It was MacLean's
organisation that was followed as the model and there is
a thread because MacLean was doing what he did best. The
dominie was spreading the word, enlightening the
unemployed that the answers lay in organising, yes, but
also in understanding the word of Charlie Marx to
liberate themselves. To paraphrase MacLean himself, it
was the application of Wee Free methods to current
political conditions and while the Wee and United Frees
were singing their psalms in the language of the garden
of Eden up in the islands regardless of what the
established Kirk might think so did John MacLean do what
he did best regardless of what the CPGB might think. He
continued to run his classes under the guise of the

Scottish Labour College to supplement what would pass as an income for him although not for much longer.

McShane gives the extent of MacLean's contribution through anecdote:

"John MacLean was a great man for the unemployed. He and I used to walk along Great Western Road on a Sunday morning at nine o'clock to the churches. We wanted to try and get into the churches to protest. And I remember one morning we were going along the road and John says to me, 'Go into the Church of England cathedral. [St Mary's near Kelvinbridge] I've got a class.' So I said, 'You'd better go to your class.' And I took the marchers. But when we got there the church people said, 'Are you going to worship?' I said, 'In to protest about unemployment.' The door was shut. We didn't get in! I felt relieved then!" (25)

MacLean just did not stop. Up out of his bed every Sunday morning to trek from Pollokshaws to Kelvinbridge in order to agitate with the Christians on a core Christian message. He had a banner specially made for the marchers: *1914 - Fighting; 1921 - Starving.*

He was jailed again in May 1921. For sedition funnily enough. His activities among the miners in Lanarkshire primarily had marked him out as the miners were still a strongly organised union and the last thing the State needed was a revolutionary preaching resistance to wage cuts. It was at this trial, which McShane reported in *The Socialist* that MacLean made his famous, simple yet powerful definition of revolution:

"The Fiscal, cross examining, questioned MacLean about what he meant by revolution. MacLean held out both hands, one above the other, he said they represented the two classes in society, the top one being the capitalist class. He then swung his hands round to the reverse position and said that was revolution." (26)

No sooner was he out of jail than he was back in the dock in October. His activities among the unemployed continued and his passion and anger over spilled again: "If Sandy Ross is a sedition monger then Lord Provost Paxton is a murderer for allowing the unemployed to starve on the streets of Glasgow." (This was part of the 3rd charge against him)

The fourth charge related to a speech in Stanley Street on 19th September. To defeat the capitalist class and their Army, Navy and Police then…" we must have unity. We must do as the Irish have done. We must vote them out of it…I hope we will be as brave as the Irish and fight together. We must fight until we have a Republic for Scotland." The charge related that this was the speech intended to cause popular disaffection. All the prosecution witnesses were police while MacLean produced none in his defence. The trial lasted 11 hours. (27)

He was jailed again for sedition which would be his fifth and last jail term. Five jail terms in his 44 years of life. This was vindictive treatment and I have no doubt that MacLean's continuing solidarity work with Irish republicans at this stage when the War of Independence was nearing completion marked him out. The rest of the Left were talking and writing – MacLean was doing (whatever that doing might have been) and the British State knew this. He made reference to Ireland again in his speech from the dock.

18 months in Barlinnie prison was the sentence. The criminal papers indicate that he refused food while on remand in Duke Street prison and drunk only tea but seemed to relent when he got to Barlinnie. Incredibly a common theme for each prison sentence that John MacLean received (apart from the vindictiveness of the sentence) was the amount of letters from various groupings throughout England and South Wales protesting his sentence and calling for his release. The letters are there preserved in the criminal papers for each sentence. This came to the attention of the Government

in London and the Commander in Chief Foster wrote to the Private Secretary to the Prime Minister recommending that his sentence of 18 months should stand – it was not his first offence. He quoted the jury's unanimous verdict that, "the words as libelled were used by the pannel and were calculated to excite popular disaffection, commotion, and resistance to lawful authority, but that it was not the pannel's intention to incite to violence." Under Scots law to prove sedition they did not have to prove intention only that tumult and violence "were the likely consequences." The letters from the "various Labour bodies" were acknowledged but not replied to. (28)

So the Government held to this line and he served a year in the east end of Glasgow. When he came out of Barlinnie for the last time in October 1922 and made his way down Cumbernauld Road for the tram back into the city he would have meditated on the fact that he no longer had either the Tramp Trust Unlimited nor the job with the Scottish Labour College. Times would be very tight indeed for MacLean as witnessed by his Poor Relief application while on remand in September 1921. The authorities marked his application with "SOCIALIST" in bold and red lettering at the top of the application which was reminiscent of the way that poor relief applications from trouble makers were handled during the Clearances. Gael had truly gone full circle. He had allies in the Socialist Labour Party and most of his writing and activity until the end of the year were conducted through the pages of *The Socialist*. He continued to correspond with his friend James Clunie who lived up in Fife. Clunie was also a tutor in the Scottish Labour College and would in later years become a Labour MP.

In late 1922 there was some form of reconciliation going on between himself and Agnes. He knew that he had to get a job and get back into teaching which he did best. He tried to get back in to the schools but was refused. This personal loss was worse than any political loss. In

a lovely letter to Jean and Nan on 26 October 1922 he
wrote:

"I was so very, very sorry that the wicked men who kept
me a prisoner wouldn't let you in to see me, although
you had come so far expecting to get in. I've heard
wonderful stories how you are both growing so big I'm
just a wee bit afraid that if you don't come home soon
again I won't know you… What a funny world it would be
if no man in the Moon came out at night to smile at the
fairies dancing round the trees in the meadows." (29)

The vindictiveness of the State carried on and on but
what is striking is the tenderness of the language. His
heart ached with missing his wee girls and Agnes was
still there giving the emotional support he needed. It
was the humanity in these letters that made John MacLean
who he was.

I am struck by the tone of his post - prison articles in
The Socialist. In the November edition John wrote an
article on *The First Great Pacific Conference of Powers*.
(30) While in jail MacLean had followed developments on
this conference in Honolulu. His grasp of international
affairs is impressive and his tone and manner were
relaxed and humorous for someone who had just come
through 5 prison stints. He referred to his stint in
"Barlinnie Hydro" at Wee Geordie's leisure and some of
his old self as Gael the columnist came out in reference
to the Conference agenda:

"If that agenda is not enough to make old Karl Marx give
an extra twang to his harp on the other side of Jordania
then I'm an apostate from Marxism." (31)

MacLean could see that the powers were jockeying for
position in the new world order. He may have got the
protagonists wrong but not the outcome of another war.
The Americans were planning a pan-American conference
for Spring 1923 with the British responding with a
Commonwealth conference and the Japanese making their
plans.

PARISH OF GLASGOW. No. 77 0011

APPLICATION FOR RELIEF. S 2768

Prison Commissioners Case

Name, *John McLean*

Residence, *Duke St. Prison*   Rent,   No. of Apartments,

Hour and Date of Application, *29/9/21*   Hour and Date of Visit,

County and Place of Birth, and if
in Scotland, Parish of Birth,

Age, *42* Condition, *Married*   Occupation, *School Teacher* Religion, *Prot.*

If Married, when, where, and by whom

Proof of Marriage,

Wholly or Partially Disabled,   Disablement as certified,

Earnings, Means, and Resources besides Parochial Relief,

Wholly or Partially Destitute,

Parentage,

Name, Age, Birthplace, and Parentage of *Wife* (or *Husband*),

Name, Age, and Birthplace of *Child* or *Children* living in family, and their earnings,

Sister Anno Maxon 39½ Pollock St. Pollokshields

Have the above had any "Clothing," "Food," "Holiday" from outside source ; if so, state particulars,

If Member of Church Mission.

Last Employer,   Wage,

Whether Husband Member of Trade Union or Friendly Society,

FOR CHILDREN NOT LIVING IN FAMILY SEE OTHER SIDE.

How was Applicant previously supported,

No. of previous applications, if any,   Nature and Parish of Settlement,

How disposed of, with Date, *29/9/21 Duke St Ob. Ward, J. Manuerman Assistant Inspector.*
1/10/21 To Prison Duke St

It all backed up his view on the, "preparations for the next day." The old dominie came out in him as he concluded in Marxian, Protestant style:

"Watch oil, watch finance but mainly watch everything vital to the social procession. Here endeth the lesson."

In the 'Hydro' he was persuaded to attend the Church service by the Assistant Chaplain, the Reverent William Fulton. He was registered as a Quaker but attended the Kirk service. Nan takes the conventional view that he went to break the monotony of prison life which is the most plausible explanation. But why would someone who had spent his adult life rejecting the 'lies' and 'hypocrisy' of organised religion just go along and listen at the back to the 'word of God'? It underestimates the fact that he graduated from the Free Church Teacher training college. MacLean knew a thing or two about what was being said and the theology behind it. It was personal reflection which seemed to calm him if the tone of his article is anything to go by. He obviously listened too if the references to the other side of Jordan and here endeth the lesson are anything to go by.

It might not equate to Connolly taking Holy Communion before his execution but I see it as really significant in bringing some threads together as to John MacLean's personal identity. MacLean was an agnostic not an atheist. He was always interested in the political interventions of organised religion and had always critiqued them. Yet when he needed some calm and serenity in his life away from his books on philosophy and poetry and the classics he returned to some old themes to focus his mind.

165

Parliamentary Election, November 15, 1922

John Maclean's

Election Address

To the Electors of
The Gorbals Division, Glasgow
The Wage-Slaves of Scotland, and
The Wage-Slaves of the British Empire

THE KEY-NOTE:
World Communism
or a
Rapidly Approaching World War

Every Vote and all Support for me means the choice of

World Communism rather than World War

MacLean's general election leaflet of November 1922 in typically uncompromising language (Courtesy - Gallacher Memorial Library)

But politics came calling again - the election of November 1922 that would see the breakthrough of the Labour Party in Glasgow and the west becoming the famous Red Clydesiders. The Communist Party too entered the fray and Willie Gallacher took on Winston Churchill up in Dundee.

MacLean was still in the Gorbals as he had been four years before and stood as an independent or as he put it not so snappily, "as a Bolshevik, alias a Communist alias a revolutionist, alias a Marxian." It's not going to get you a date on a modern dating website is it but there was logic. MacLean saw himself as the true standard bearer. The election campaign unleashed all the old energy that exhilarated him but would destroy him too.

"For twenty years I have been a socialist and have devoted the best of my energy to convert workers to socialism and to teach Marx's writings on wealth production and the course and meaning of historical development during that period." (32)

This was never an election address in any sense of the term. It was a personal manifesto and a personal story of how he had stuck to his Red Flag and fought through the betrayals and hardship. He emphasised his personal credentials as a revolutionary and, indeed, he accompanied this election address with two leaflets – Red Flag flutters and the re-issued All hail, the Scottish Workers Republic! – and a personal explanation of his address. The good people of the Gorbals had plenty of reading material. What comes out are his thoughts on Scotland, the international situation, his views on a coming war between new imperialists all in machine gun fashion.

There are two striking elements though. The Red and the Green were worn side by side. As Ireland was embarking on its post Treaty, partitionist journey MacLean wrote:

"The cruel torture of Ireland has largely ruined Ireland already." (33)

A key section of the Red Flag Flutters leaflet is given to the hypocrisy of the British position in Ireland and

the continuing mischief of Edward, now Lord, Carson.
Students of Irish history will know of this privileged
Dublin boy's role in stirring up the north eastern
counties of Ireland which played a huge part in the
notion of partitioning Ireland into two statelets. As a
result of the Treaty Ireland had a Free State but six
counties became 'Northern Ireland' and stayed in the UK.
Just for the record that is what happened to a country
who returned 75% of their MP's as Republicans in the
last general election at a time when the democracies of
the West were preaching self-determination. MacLean knew
this and predicted more mischief from Carson. (34)

The second element is his unilateral adoption of the,
"Sinn Fein tactics." Of course, Scotland was not
Ireland. There was not even a nationalist party
contesting the election. Yet MacLean stood out:

"To get a Scottish Workers Republic I shall not go to
the London House of Commons but stay in Scotland helping
the unemployed, standing by those at work, educating in
the Scottish Labour College and carrying revolutionary
propaganda all over Scotland (and into England too.)"
(35)

An extreme viewpoint but wasn't extremity a virtue?
MacLean's point was simple. The Imperial Parliament was
no place for a Scottish Socialist to be. You could
achieve nothing there. MacLean lost the election to
George Buchanan, the Labour candidate who was one of the
twenty two MP's who left St Enoch train station in
December 1922 bound for Westminster. In a nod to the
tradition that they were leaving behind the
Internationale was sung along with some Gaelic psalms
and other socialist songs. The new MP's genuinely
believed that they were going to make a difference.

They were leaving the tradition behind. They were
embarking on the journey which the CP would articulate
as the British road to socialism. Labour Party
supporters will of course claim that they made

achievements. That is a different debate for a different book.

But it is significant that one of the best fighters in the Labour camp – James Maxton – was soon disillusioned. He had been a pupil at MacLean's economics classes and certainly made a name for himself by upsetting the etiquette of Parliament. But his experience would soon make him adopt language that was not unlike MacLean's as he sought to turn the, "English ridden, capitalist ridden, landlord ridden Scotland into the Scottish Socialist Commonwealth." (36) This was in 1924 so the novelty that was Westminster had quickly worn off. In August, the Labour MP's (including Maxton, Tom Johnston, Buchanan and Neil McLean) attended a Home Rule demonstration at the William Wallace memorial at Robroyston near Glasgow. The speeches denounced English domination, the English House of commons and they resolved to carry on the fight for, "an independent Parliament" even if it meant a fight like that of Ireland's. (37)

The Clydeside Labour MP's battled on moving many Home Rule bills until they fizzled out in the early thirties. Nationalist sentiments were equated with the rising fascist movement and they were whipped into line to get back on the British road to socialism. Maxton couldn't stomach it.

Tactically, MacLean's call for abstentionism was a non-starter with no movement behind him as Sinn Fein had. But his poser a year later "Had the labour men stayed in Glasgow…" certainly raises questions as to the degeneration of the Red Clydeside into an electoral machine churning out Party hacks from safe Labour seats and hoping that England would return enough MP's to form governments.

It is worthy of note that MacLean polled over 4000 votes in the November 1922 election – the "Red and Green supporters of a Scottish Workers Republic" that he alluded to the Irish Taoiseach. He wanted to bring these forces together and so formed his own party in April 1923 - the Scottish Workers Republican Party. He had support through a personal following and Constance Markievicz and Jim Larkin and Sylvia Pankhurst all spoke for him on his council hustings. As Tommy Sheridan and Alan McCombes, have written it was the SWRP that was the first pro-independence political party in Scotland predating the Scottish Party and the National Party of Scotland who would come together to form the SNP eleven years later. (38)

It is significant that by his last general election campaign which dismayed and angered Agnes that he could do that to himself again, so soon after the last one, he stood as one of a few SWRP candidates and signed himself: John MacLean, MA - Republican.

A Scottish Republican. How did the Communist machine react to this?

I remember Alexei Sayle, the "Marxist comedian" whose parents had been Communists, talking about Stalin touch up jobs on paintings. This was the phenomena that added Stalin to historic paintings to enhance his revolutionary reputation. Sayle said his favourite one was the one where Stalin scored the winning goal for Coventry in the 1949 FA Cup final! Uncle Joe could also make people disappear - they could become non-persons.

For a while in true Stalinist, pre Stalin, style MacLean became a non-person. His Party were denounced as "claymore communists." There was no political debate with MacLean's position or Party. It was all about trivialising and marginalising John MacLean to the point where they believed that he posed no political threat. He didn't live to see the 1923 general election so he didn't live to see Ramsay MacDonald's first Labour government. He died on St Andrews Day. Gallacher wrote an obituary in *The Communist International*. It is undated but must have been December 1923 or at the latest January 1924. His shock is genuine as was his praise for MacLean's contribution yet there was no

mention of his political critique of the CP and his call
for a Workers Republic. (39)

This set the tone for the Communist Party's dualism in
the years that followed. He was hero and villain; brave
yet a dupe; brave fighter and mad all at different
times. It was a continuation of the tone set while he
was living. In the 1920's and early thirties the CP
still had competition from the SWRP (which existed until
the early thirties) and from Guy Aldred's anarchists.
(40) When the threat had nullified MacLean moved out of
being a non-person. Gallacher wrote of him in similar
terms to his obituary in Revolt on the Clyde (his own
memoirs) and returned to the persecution complex theory.

A full CP biography came out - the second biography of
MacLean (41) written by Tom Bell which was subtitled *A
Fighter for Freedom*. Again, this is a genuine biography
in many respects. There are many poignant reminiscences
and stories and Bell begins by writing that John
belonged to, "the great family of Communism." (42) Yet
amid the real understanding of a comrade - former
comrade - who lived and breathed the struggle, time had
not softened the blow of the split that occurred. There
was no empathy or even political rebuff to MacLean's
line. Instead there was the insinuation:

"This was not the real MacLean speaking, but a man who
had suffered much, and who was no longer seeing things
in the proper perspective, due to the warping of his
better judgement." (43)

To be specific and to the point, he wasn't seeing the
CPGB line in "the proper perspective." The mud stuck
and many on the British Left saw persecution complexes
and hallucinations caused by years of prison which led
to off the wall theories and writings. They don't see
the tenderness in his letters to his daughters, the
rationalism in his letters to Clunie. They choose not to
see his political critique of a Party that was embarking
on a subservient, pro-Russian road that would haunt them
in later years:

171

"In spite of my keen desire to go to Russia, in spite of my equally keen desire to help Lenin and the other comrades I am not prepared to let Moscow dictate to Glasgow. The Communist party has sold itself to Moscow with disastrous results to both Russia and the British revolutionary movement." (44)

MacLean wrote this in 1922. He was right in both his critique and in his decision not to join the new Party. He could never have foreseen that the gramophones of Lenin would become the gramophones of Stalin. They would perform ideological cartwheels in the thirties and forties that MacLean could not have done. But he did see the writing on the wall as the CP uncritically mimicked the Russian Party and he saw other good comrades being marginalised namely Sylvia Pankhurst and Jim Larkin too.

For all the Communist Party may have wanted to lay claim to the legend of John MacLean they could not square this political circle. The mantle fell to poets and songwriters – in all the tongues of Scotland – to keep alive his politics and his memory. Hugh MacDiarmid believed that communism in Scotland was, "poisoned at its very well spring by this betrayal of John MacLean." (45) Kendall puts it powerfully:

"From the 1930's the Party has seen fit to allow MacLean to appear as the spiritual father of the Party in Scotland. The fact that whilst he was alive the same Party hierarchy was opposing his political activity and pursuing him to his grave with unfounded accusations of mental 'instability' brings little but discredit on the originators of the accusations…" (46)

Uncle Joe Stalin would take this to extremes with his murderous purges in the 1930's with not a mention of paranoia from his gramophones in the CP. Maybe they didn't know. Poor old Willie, poor old Tom, poor old Harry McShane who needed Soviet tanks in Hungary in 1956 to waken him up.

172

As for poor old John he was above this and he kept true to his principles as he had done all his life even if it meant he was on the losing side. Ain't that the way with principled people? Inspiring, legendary, visionary and worth a song or two but he still lost. Sadly, as any good political cynic will tell you, it's not about principles but power and ego and jostling for position and these were all things that John MacLean wasn't good at. Spare a thought for poor old Alexander Dubcek who was in charge of Czechoslovakia in the late 1960's. He gave Communism in the Soviet Bloc a life line; a chance to adapt to a vision of socialist democracy. He had vision among vision-less bureaucrats.

"We consider socialist democracy to be a system in which the working man has his own standing and value, his security, his right, and his future. It is based upon human participation, coherence, and cooperation. We wish to meet people's longing that they can feel to be human among humans. This active, humane, integrating part of socialism, a society without antagonism, that is what we want to realise systematically and gradually, serving the people." (47)

This was a vision that MacLean the teacher could relate to. The response? The Russians invaded in 1968 to quell the Prague Spring initiated by this libertarian thought and Dubcek was taken away in a car. Ain't that the way with principled people?

NOTES

1) Matt McGinn, The Treasure Chest, undated collection of poems/songs.

2) For an excellent account of the saga please see Walter Kendall, *The Revolutionary Movement in Britain 1900 - 21*, 1969, chapter 17.

3) Quoted in Kendall, op cit.

4) Tom Bell, *John MacLean: A Fighter for Freedom*, 1944, p.107.

5) Jim Clayson, *John MacLean and Conspiracies*, Scottish Workers Republic, An Geamradh/Winter, 2004.

6) Willie Gallacher, *Revolt on the Clyde*, 1936.

7) David Burke, *Theodore Rothstein and Russian Political Émigré Influence on the British Labour Movement, 1884 - 1920*, Greenwich University thesis, 1997, p.190-1.

8) Barbara Winslow, *Sylvia Pankhurst: Sexual politics and political activism*, 1996, p. 164

9) John MacLean, *A Scottish Communist Party*, December 1920 in In the Rapids of Revolution, 1973, p. 225

10)   See James D. Young, John MacLean: Clydeside Socialist, 1991, p.233

11)   Bell, ibid, p. 110

12)   Kendall, ibid, p.286

13)   See, for example Dave Sherry, *John Maclean - Red Clydesider*, 2014. Dave manages to write a chapter on MacLean and the CPGB asserting the reasons why John didn't join as well as the reasons why he was tactically wrong without a single quote from MacLean himself!

14)   Winslow, ibid, p.169

15)   Bell, ibid., p. 110

16)   Winslow, ibid, p.170

17)   VI Lenin, *Left Wing Communism: An Infantile Disorder*, in …. It is interesting that Gallacher too is criticised in this polemic but he quickly became the apparatchik.

18)   I have previously argued that it was a tactical mistake but see it differently now. See

Gerry Cairns, *Why John MacLean did not join the Communist Party of Great Britain*, Scottish Workers Republic, An t-Earrach/Spring 2005

19)   Quoted in Winslow, ibid, p.174
20)   MacLean, "A Scottish Communist Party", December 1920, *In the Rapids of Revolution*, p. 224
21)   MacLean, ibid., p.225
22)   John Henderson, *Moscow and the SLP*, The Socialist, March 1923.
23)   *Open Letter to Lenin* (30 January 1921), in MacLean, ibid., p.228.
24)   Burke thesis, 1997, p. 268
25)   MacLean, ibid. p. 229
26)   Harry McShane in Ian MacDougall (ed.) *Voices from the Hunger Marches, Volume 1*, 1990, p. 16
27)   Quoted in MacLean, ibid p. 233
28)   John MacLean criminal papers, HH116/122.
29)   John MacLean, *The Socialist*, November 1922.
30)   Criminal papers, Ibid.
31)   MacLean, ibid., p.250-1.
32)   Election address, November 1922 in MacLean, ibid. p 234.
33)   MacLean, ibid. p.237
34)   Red Flag Flutters, November 1922, in MacLean ibid. p240
35)   Election address, November 1922, in MacLean ibid. p. 238
36)   See Gordon Brown, *Maxton*, 1988, p.161
37)   *Scotland's Day – A Glasgow Pageant*, Glasgow Herald, 27/8/23
38)   Alan McCombes and Tommy Sheridan, *Imagine: A Socialist Vision for the 21st Century*, 2000
39)   Willie Gallacher, *John MacLean*, The Communist International, No.30
40)   The Anti-Parliamentary Communist Federation.
41)   After Comrade Tom Anderson's book.
42)   Bell, Ibid. p. 11
43)   Bell, ibid. p. 124
44)   MacLean, ibid. p241

45)   Hugh MacDiarmid, *John MacLean*, The Word, n.d
  originally printed in December 1940
46)   Kendall, ibid. p. 291
47)   Alexander Dubcek, Speech to the Communist
  Party of Czechoslovakia, 1st April 1968, *Blueprint
  for Freedom*, 1969 p 74.

POSTCRIPT - THE PARTY ON MacLEAN

The Soviet Communist Party had an extensive team of
researchers who supported the publication of the
classics of Marxism-Leninism, as it became. All the
classics of Marxist literature were published in the
western countries in the main languages and sold as
cheap as chips. There were always extensive footnotes
giving the Party line on every conceivable subject while
heroising the good guys in almost saintly language and
vilifying the bad guys in almost hateful terms. Not
surprisingly who was good and who was bad could change
and the footnotes changed accordingly.

Lenin's non-person of 1920, his first appointed Consul
in Scotland, got a mention in the publication of Lenin's
Selected Works in 1977 published in the USSR:

"John Maclean (1879 - 1923) - a prominent leader of the
British labour movement. Prior to the First World War
joined the left wing of the British Socialist Party and
became one of its leaders in Scotland. During the First
World War adopted an internationalist stand."

And that is it. Maybe he really died in 1918. Maybe he
disappeared for the last five years of his life. Or
rather with the passage of time the post Stalin scribes
still couldn't bring themselves to acknowledge the
contribution of their former Consul for the last five
years of his life. 50 years after his death, the Party
was still right and John MacLean was still wrong.

Soviet Commemorative stamp

CONCLUSION — The Politics of Failure or the Failure of Politics?

"What invigorates life invigorates death,

And the dead advance as much as the living advance,

And the future is no more uncertain than the present,

And the roughness of the earth and of man encloses as

Much as the delicatesse of the earth and of man,

And nothing endures but personal qualities."

   - Walt Whitman (1)

"Make up your minds beforehand not to worry about how you will defend yourselves because I will give you such words and wisdom that none of your enemies will be able to refute or contradict what you say."

   - Jesus Christ (2)

Pneumonia was the cause of death. That bout of pneumonia struck MacLean down during the General Election of 1923: the election that would lead to the formation of the first Labour Government in Westminster. He passed away on November 30th 1923. Tom Anderson bore witness:

"Two days before the nomination day I received from him in an envelope marked 'Comrade Tom Anderson', £25, which I had given him as part of the £150 deposit. Comrade John's wife brought it to me and I knew something serious was wrong." (3)

It was Tom Anderson himself who conducted the funeral service and he estimated that about 10000 followed the funeral led by the Clyde Workers Silver Band with children from the Proletarian Sunday School. Anderson recalled "Comrade Richard Lee" making the oration while

the Glasgow Citizen reported a "Reverent Richard Lee"
with a photograph of him clearly standing in the middle
of the crowd in what looks like religious garb. Was
there a religious component to MacLean's funeral
service? The Reverent Lee had written a pamphlet that
was reviewed by MacLean back in February 1920 (4) He is
cited as the most "outspoken clergyman in Scotland" and
was resident at that time in Dundee. Did Agnes insist on
a religious component to the ceremony? In prison in 1917
John had written his sister with tongue firmly in cheek
to tell Agg that, "I remember her in my prayers!!!" Was
this a gentle tease at his wife's faith?

Of course the holy Reverend may have come of his own
volition as a socialist leaning minister but it is hard
to believe that he did not bury MacLean in the presence
of his God. Lee in his pamphlet had defended Bolshevism
although it is worth a pause to reflect that he
qualified this by stating that it was the "spirit of
revolution" not their specific war methods. Lee, unlike
MacLean, was a pacifist and he asserted:

"The present form of society whether in economics,
government or religion is based on the obsolete
principle of selfishness and tribal hate. The organic
law of human society for the world today is that of
mutual cooperation."

Not many would define their Marxism like this as it is
more akin to the old Social Democracy than
contemporaneous Bolshevism. MacLean was one of the few
who concurred and probably speaks more about MacLean's
'Bolshevism' than his left wing, minister friend.

By the time of the funeral the Reverend Lee was based in
Ross Street Unitarian Church in the Calton in Glasgow.
It is certainly true that Lee stayed true to his
socialist and pacifist principles through to the break
out of the next War when he defended political
conscientious objectors. He stated "that it was amazing
that men of scholarship and intellect should uphold the
distinction between a political CO and a religious CO,

and proceed to condemn the conscience of a political CO
as mere cowardice, while accepting the conscience of a
Plymouth Brethren or Christadelphian. It is assumed that
a man's conscience is regarded as having some relation
to an ethical religion. If the CO can quote from the
Bible, he has a greater chance of remaining on the valid
CO list."

Of course, it was a secular service and there was
certainly nothing religious in the music as the crowd
sang *A Rebel Song*, *The Red Flag* and concluded with the
Internationale. Tom Anderson would have ensured that
the funeral ran like a socialist Sunday school!

Agnes received many tributes to the house including
telegrams from Helen Crawford, Willie Gallacher who was
contesting the election in Dundee, who was, "shocked to
hear of the death of old comrade." There was also an
unsigned telegram from Greenock. (5) Scottish
nationalists paid their tribute too. A letter from E
Gillies from the London Branch of the Scots National
League hailed John's devotion to the "cause of Scots
republicanism" and called him a "true patriot":

"The ideals of freedom that he engendered in Scottish
hearts remain. To carry on, to march forward in hope and
determination toward the day when the Scottish people
should throw off the shackles of imperialism and as a
free and independent nation take their place in the
front rank of the nations striving for international
brotherhood and justice – that is the greatest tribute
we can pay to the memory of a leader and true comrade in
the cause." (6)

MacLean's comrades on Green Clydeside paid their tribute
too. There was a note from William Richardson on behalf
of the "Irish electors of the Gorbals" (7) where MacLean
was standing in order not go to Parliament and also from
Mary Murray who sent greetings, "from the Irish
Republicans of Glasgow and District." (8) Both notes
were short and sincere with Ms Murray admiring that
John, "stood for fair play and justice for all."

This photo comes from the Glasgow Citizen a week after the
funeral with the caption: "A long procession composed of
members of the various Republican organisations with which
the deceased was connected followed the remains to the
Eastwood New Cemetery where the service was taken by the Rev.
Richard Lee." The reverent appears to be in religious garb
with hand raised.

Comrade Tom kept the same format as the funeral with his
annual John MacLean march. This Order of Service dates
from 1926. (Courtesy – The Mitchell Library Glasgow
Room.)

182

The most poignant tribute came from Neil Johnston who was MacLean's friend from the West Indies. Mr Johnston was in possession of MacLean's overcoat which was given to him as a sign that Neil needed it in the cold Scottish climate more than John did. This was acknowledged as MacLean was, "one big lump of kindness and sincerity." (9) Johnston alerted us to something that did not come across in MacLean's writings – racism in sections of Scottish society. By understanding, "bias conceptions" concerning colour in Scotland, MacLean proved himself to be, "a true White Man." One can only surmise that this was the product of prejudice experienced by Neil Johnston in the West of Scotland and the words in tribute are clearly very personal. He told Agnes the he hoped that the freedom from pain through death would bring a, "brighter future for you and your little ones."

I cannot find any recorded evidence of Agnes' feelings. She was receiving political tribute after political tribute with lots of personal praise towards the warm human being that was her husband. There are no memoirs or letters that I can see that give Agnes' version. Mrs MacLean retained a dignified silence. We do know that Jean was 12 and Nan was 10 when they buried their father. There is no doubting Tom Anderson's sterling work in assisting with the fund that would raise £1713 2 shillings and 7 pence to assist the family. It would be young Nan who would stay true to her old Dad's politics. Jean we know to have kicked back against them even as a teenager. (10) This is a perfectly human reaction. How do we know and how can we judge what she thought of her father putting the Cause before his family?

John MacLean loved Agnes and his girls with all his heart. In his last letter to Agnes, he pleads with his wife to return. He writes passionately:

"Whatever course we follow remember that you are the only woman I love & can now love." (11)

It is heart-breaking. Even more so when reading the final sentence:

"Tell Nan and Jean I don't present feel in the mood to write them as I would so keenly desire to do."

He never would get the chance to write them again. It is remiss in presenting a portrait of John MacLean not to focus on this. What were his girls to think when reading this? He was exhausted – physically and mentally – and was about to throw himself into another political campaign in the Gorbals which, according to Nan, extremely angered her Mum. In the letter he expects Agnes to fall in line. Indeed it was her "duty" to stand with him in the political struggle. He just couldn't see that maybe his wife had had enough. Although he really should have shouldn't he? It is revealing that Nan quotes the last letter to her Mum at great length in her biography but leaves out the last sentence and she was entitled to her counsel on this. John Broom states that Agnes did indeed return to the family home a couple of weeks before he died but I'm not sure if this was a permanent move.

My own view is that politics was his addiction. It was more than passion and carried a destructive element as all addictions do wrecking his life at every level. As Dr Devon observed when he was in Perth prison it was visits from comrades or from his wife that got him exciteable and agitated with massive mood swings dependent upon the news given. This didn't make him mad or insane and the prison doctor did not say that he was. It was other prison administrators, civil servants and Tory and Communist politicians who said that. (12) MacLean was human – that's all – and the Cause took over his whole life. As the political morphine streamed through his veins he either couldn't see the price his family were paying or, if he did, he could not do anything about it. Not without an anti-political rehab programme! His family suffered and too many, male, writers are too blasé on this aspect of his character.

His premature death at the age of 44 in the circumstances gave him martyrdom. Tom Anderson would organise a John MacLean march every year from Eglinton Toll to the graveside in Eastwood Cemetery- the "Silent March" - which was attended by about 500 people with the commemoration following the same format as the funeral service. This march took place throughout the thirties and forties and could have been pushed along by the individual energy of Comrade Tom Anderson who saw the march as a personal debt of gratitude to MacLean.

It is unclear as to when the original John MacLean march fizzled out. Its memory would be immortalised by the Edinburgh songwriter and folklorist, Hamish Henderson in 1948. It was at a meeting of the Scotland - USSR Friendship Society and Hamish's new song was sung by William Noble as his tribute to John MacLean. He called the song, *The John MacLean March*. This was a fitting title in line with the annual commemoration to his memory but it gave the march a legendary status. This march was no longer a south Glasgow affair! Rather it was an all Scotland march with the marchers coming from the Gorgie, the Lammerlaw and even north of the Tay and I suspect that Henderson was nodding a wink to his travels back from prison. The real purpose was that MacLean himself led the march and was coming hame; hame tae the Clyde.

The socialist red and the Irish green were seen side by side along with various trades marching toward Glasgow Green and this imagery is the most striking. These colours were seen in the May Day rally in 1919, as we have seen, and here they were back together in a sort of homage to a great man. The whole crowd was silent:

"Tak' tent when he's speaking for you'll mind what he says here;

In Glesca oor city and the whale warld besides." (13)

The silence was to hear 'Hielan' Shony' who was invited back to Glasgow for his tea and some rest. The imagery of rest (death) and of being at peace with his friends in Glasgow brought the march back home in beautiful language. And that language was Scots. It built up to the crescendo of the song and was a sort of legacy of John MacLean in itself as he wrote that the "Red would be worn and Scotland will rise again when great John MacLean has come hame tae the Clyde." Scottish freedom and socialism were conjoined in the shape and memory of MacLean. This song painted a portrait of MacLean in itself. More significantly, John became the intellectual property of the singers and poets rather than the politicos.

Indeed, when Hamish would have sat down to the applause of the friends of Scotland and the USSR after Mr Noble's performance it was probably appropriate that no one dragged up old fights. It was not the time to mention that Scotland and the USSR may have been friends but the Soviet Union was no friend of MacLean shortly before he died. That was a one way friendship and the first Consul wasn't to find out that he had been dumped by Lenin and co. No hard feelings eh?

The late thirties and early forties witnessed MacLean's reinstatement in Communist Party circles. From Gallacher's obituary in January 1924 until the publication of his memoirs (Revolt on the Clyde) in 1936 it is no exaggeration to say that MacLean was a non-person. Tom Bell followed suit in 1944 with his biography. Yet the CP sought to reinstate a legend: of a fighter for the working class, a martyr, a hero who went astray. His autonomous Scottish socialism did not sit with a unified British party taking orders from Moscow and playing the game of parliamentary socialism in Westminster. Gallacher himself was an MP for Fife. Neither did his Scottish socialist vision sit with the nascent Scottish National Party founded in 1934 whose vision of independence was Home Rule with Dominion Status. His politics just didn't sit.

It is certainly true that the Scottish Workers
Republican Party continued in existence until 1932 and
along with Guy Aldred's anarchists proved to be a thorn
in the flesh of the CPGB. There was no outstanding
leader in the SWRP to replace MacLean but their politics
was a counterpoint to the Communist orthodoxy of what
would become the British Road to Socialism. They irked
the Scottish Executive of the CP enough to warrant a
nickname: the Claymore Communists. This had more irony
that they could imagine as MacLean used to whimsically
refer to Gael taking up his targe and claymore for the
industrial struggles of the Clyde when he wrote his
column for Justice just prior to the outbreak of WW1.
Aldred too got MacLean's politics. He would constantly
refer to setting up a pulpit in every part of Scotland
to preach for a Workers Scottish Republic as he called
it in his own idiosyncratic style. Neither group was
strong in terms of numbers or members but they took the
message to Glasgow Green hustings and street corners and
it is widely reported by contemporaries that the
introduction of traffic lights in the city hastened the
demise of both parties as they could no longer set up
their hustings at the street corners.

The British socialist orthodoxy went largely
unchallenged throughout the 1930's as the election of a
socialist, Labour government became the target. A
dwindling band of politicos led by Comrade Tom marched
and marched each year while new voices emerged. The poet
Hugh MacDiarmid was almost a lone voice as he argued for
a "MacLean line" as opposed to the party line in the
1930's. Hamish Henderson wrote his famous song and among
poets and singers and artists something resonated in
John MacLean. Songwriters such Morris Blythman (who also
wrote as Thurso Berwick) and Jim McLean brought
MacLean's republicanism into their many Scottish protest
songs of the 1960's coinciding with a rise in support
for the SNP. In 1968 the John MacLean Society was formed
with folkies and artists at the helm with the drive of
John's daughter, Nan, and some old comrades like Harry
McShane who had also let bygones be bygones.

If the CP's portrait of MacLean was a large part legend, then it is equally true to say that the poets and singers did likewise. Fifty years after his death in 1973 the Homage was complete. Coinciding with the release of two fine biographies (by Nan Milton and John Broom respectively) the poets gave their booklet the fitting title, *Homage to John MacLean*. A homage in poem and song that painted a portrait of MacLean as the essence and permanence of Scotland itself. MacLean is celebrated in all three languages of Gaelic, Scots and English. The editors, especially in line with Blythman's view, felt that MacLean united the "national and international sense of the Scottish people." They were pretty clear, unequivocal even, in their rationale for this homage:

"By following the example of MacDiarmid, the poets contribute to the re-establishment of MacLean as a figure of epic significance. In the matter of whom do we remember and how do we remember him, the poets always have the last word, something politicians among others should always remember." (14)

Among an impressive array of poets and powerful poetry there is one little poem by Tom Scott that seems to summarise MacLean and yet provoke our thoughts too as to who he was and is:

"Marx your faither, your mither was the Clyde.

You, throu aa your life, were true to them baith..

Whaur they conflictit, it was hard to side

Wi' either, and atween the twae, in fear and faith

You struggled tae manhood. Lenin set the pace

And the socialist world was set in a Russian mould.

The only pattern, it seemed for the human race:

Ither lands tae be sheep in the Russian fold.

But the Clyde maun find its ain wey oot tae sea

And you, like Marx nae Marxist, glegly saw

(As Broz did later in Yugoslavia)

That ilka land its national weird maun dree:

Sae wi Marx's tools you wrocht the Scottish nation

A socialism for Scotland's ain salvation." (15)

This is eulogy and challenge in one short poem that captures movingly his break with British Socialism and Russia with his vision for Scotland. The reference to Karl Marx's famous statement that he was no Marxist is a challenge to those on the Left. MacLean may have called himself a Bolshevik but was he really? We can all say and believe things about ourselves but it does not make them true. In practice and in tactics, the poet saw something different to what the political apparatchik would see. It is an appropriate challenge while it is of course true that the poets added a large dollop of romance to the portrait of John MacLean.

A few years later, the respected journalist Neal Ascherson wrote on the 'cult' of MacLean. He felt that MacLean's "faith in enlightenment to bring revolution" actually placed him closer to Rosa Luxemburg than to Lenin stating that John could not have accepted democratic centralism. (16) In being critical of the cult Ascherson also challenges us to think of MacLean differently. While Hugh MacDiarmid, for all his fine writings, would have us see MacLean as a Scottish Lenin, the truth is that MacLean was no such thing and that brings his politics to the fore.

It is too easy to convey the politics as that of failure – either from the British Left or mainstream Scottish nationalism. The politics of isolation or of extremes but it all ends up in the same place: failure. His supporters then sing a song while his detractors tell us he was mad while MacLean's politics have been crowded out. That is why he is a kind of folk hero, a sentence or two in most generalist histories of Scotland.

Has MacLean left a political legacy? It is a bit disingenuous to say that his legacy is that of a revolutionary Marxist. For starters John MacLean was not an original Marxist thinker and did not add to the canon of literature. He was a dominie and took Marxian economics to the working class. That was his most significant contribution. There is also the small matter of not actually having been involved in any workers' revolution! He undoubtedly wanted one and articulated what it would actually mean but the British State believed that there would be a revolution more than what the workers did as was witnessed by the bemused reaction to tanks appearing in Glasgow in January 1919. As we have seen he was involved in a revolution but it was a nationalist one to free Ireland.

His real political legacy for me was in his break with British socialism and adoption of a Scottish republican position – the MacLean line. This was contentious and still provokes debate today. This was original in that he took what he believed was a Marxist position on the Scottish national question. This republican position is what still sets him apart today. I have argued that MacLean was no Saul on the Road to Damascus. (17) Many factors contributed to his promotion of Scottish independence. The debate around national self-determination at the end of the First World War within the Scottish Left; the events in Ireland; the direction that the British Left were taking all played significant parts. They swirled around in his head at a time of huge flux in his own life. Gael came home to the political position that the indigenous Left in Scotland should always have taken. As Scottish socialists in a British organisation they were always trained to be parochial and to ignore what their heart was telling them. They could only be internationalist by being British. MacLean broke this mould. He wanted neither London nor Moscow to run his Party and asked the question: why can't Scotland have her own organisation in the great socialist international?

I suppose that is why it is called the national question. John MacLean combined the national and social questions into a position that he felt would liberate his class and his country. There is no doubting that he lost the debate but this does not mean that he was not ahead of his time. He never called himself a Scottish nationalist although he used language that was nationalist to his old comrades on the Left.

It is important to the modern Left who are at pains to point out that MacLean was no nationalist. No way José! This would signify John going over to the other side. So they block out his language and imagery of "brother Celts", "Highland and Scottish traditions" as well as journeys to Arbroath to celebrate, albeit with idiosyncratic reasons, a declaration of Scottish independence. I think that you would be called a Scottish nationalist if you came out with such views.

For me, I don't think he was a nationalist. He forged an alliance with left leaning nationalists to further the cause of a pro-independence Party of the Left. This probably explains why he has had minimal impact on the wider Scottish nationalist movement and the growth of the SNP. As James Hunter put it:

"But it is undoubtedly the case that neither the Gaelic Scotland of Erskine nor the workers' republic of MacLean figure prominently in modern Scottish nationalism." (18)

Both figures are too extreme for a gradualist movement that is seeking to win a very different kind of independent Scotland.

However, as the twentieth century came to a close various Left organisations in Scotland re-examined their political relationship with Britain and saw a Scottish road to socialism. A united Scottish Socialist Party arose and had electoral impact in the Scottish Parliament. John MacLean's socialist republic was an inspiration and many of the leaders of the SSP acknowledged this. The SSP's rise and fall in the 1990's and early 2000's is not our concern here. Yet with that party's rise a genie came out of a bottle for British socialism north of the border and it wasn't going back inside that bottle. Why shouldn't Scotland have its own socialist party? Didn't MacLean say that back in the 1920's? Well yes, he did!

The queer folk of the Shaws would waken up to a John MacLean March again every November and they still do thanks to the sterling work of another Mr Anderson – Donald Anderson and a small band of republican socialists.

It is of course true that today John MacLean is a marginal, cult figure but that has been by design through a failure of politics. A politics that was about a Party machine that drowned out revisionist voices such as Pankhurst, Larkin or MacLean. A politics that did what it was told by Moscow which then told its members to do what they were told. They called it democratic centralism. Google it you are interested. It is as far removed from Charlie Marx as TV Evangelists are from the gentle Christ. MacLean was a victim of this failure of politics.

Some may argue that he should have adapted and went with the tide. Perhaps. Yet it was in his nature to do what he thought was right. Yet the key failure of politics is that there is little room for principle. You need to adapt to the mainstream – whatever – that mainstream may be or you 'die.' This failure consumed his enemies too. Jim McLean is a well-known figure in Scottish folk music circles and part of the folk revival that had Peace and

Republicanism at its heart in the 1960's. Jim recounted this story to me regarding Willie Gallacher which I quote in full as anecdotal history:

"I met Willy Gallagher sometime around 1963. We are/were both from Paisley and I visited him at his home in Rowan Street. I seem to remember one had to pull a cord of some sort to access his bedroom up a flight of internal stairs as he was bedridden.
My young brother Wallace, who was an apprentice baker was with me and Willy gave him a book on baking as they seemed to have a common interest in that subject.
Being a McLean I asked him about John MacLean and he said he had a "falling out" with him but in the light of today's political circumstances he said he would agree with MacLean now. I asked him if he thought MacLean had become mad, or mentally unstable as had been mooted by others. He didn't think MacLean had any mental problems but that the British Establishment had treated him "brutally". I mentioned that I had served a six-month sentence in Barlinnie as a Conscientious Objector against the Suez fiasco. "That's nothing" he said. "I have been jailed three times!"
I was writing Scottish Republican songs at the time and he was very sympathetic to the idea of a Republican Scotland but thought it would be an uphill struggle as the British Establishment was "very devious".
I never visited him again as I was moving back and forth from Scotland to Europe and he died soon afterwards, but from his mood and conciliatory attitude to John MacLean, I felt he would be supporting Scottish Independence now."

It seems an about turn from the Gallacher that MacLean was talking about in 1920. Yet Gallacher did what he did and said what he said for his Party - his Party right or wrong. Maybe his own Westminster experience was similar to Jimmy Maxton and this led him to see the MacLean line in a different light. It certainly puts politics in a certain light for this author.

Yet even though Gallacher's CP machine took over the work that he was doing with the unemployed it did not diminish MacLean's passion. In a supplement in The Socialist in December 1922 he set out a utopian scheme:

"In Glasgow I am proposing that within the next year over £26 million ought to be spent in re-claiming Mearns Moor and other waste land round the city along scientific lines and that experiments in colony or communal methods of land cultivation ought to be carried out on a large scale sufficient to absorb the 30000 and more at present unemployed." (19)

John was just out of prison where he had costed what in effect would become public works schemes in the 1930's for a specific part of Glasgow. The problem, however, was inherent in Left politics. MacLean was certainly not unique in coming out with ideas, viable or not. There were plenty of issues, weekly class struggles but no coherent vision of what Socialism would look like.

It wasn't there in Marx or Engels. There was a critique of the present system but not much on what would replace it. The great Social Democracy was held up before World War 1; Communism after the revolution in Russia. The former was betrayed by political opportunism; the latter was the betrayer of many hopes, ideals and the murderer of millions who held those hopes and ideals.

It is no accident that MacLean the Social Democrat was more positive, more whimsical and more influential as the Dominie. Of course, the War and imprisonment took their toll as did his political addiction after the end of the war. I refer to the fact that as many today are reverting to talk of "social democratic politics", which usually means moderate, left of centre politics, then perhaps a fitting tribute to the legacy of John MacLean would be to re-examine the great Social Democracy. Go back to the first principles of what we are trying to build. That is what contemporaries remembered about John MacLean: the teacher at the factory gate preaching the great Social Democracy. Just a thought.

When I think of how politics consumed MacLean and how
the Left helped to break him I am struck again by Neal
Ascherson's comparison with Rosa Luxemburg, the Polish
born revolutionary who was killed by a right wing
militia in early 1919 in Germany. In one of her prison
letters she was full of a longing for nature. She was
not like "bankrupt politicians." She wasn't "treasonable
to socialism" by feeling more at home in her garden than
at a party congress. She prophesied that she would, "die
at her post…a street fight or in prison" but, "my
innermost personality belongs more to my tomtits than to
the comrades." (20)

In MacLean's more tender moments there is a comparison
in articulating such thoughts. Some letters from his
last stints in prison show this streak. In a letter to
his sister, Lizzie he asks her to get a gardener if the
place is in "bad order." In a letter dated 27th September
1922 to "my dear Pietro" (most probably Peter Marshall)
he jokes, "I expect to blossom as a street artist on my
release" asking Pietro not to give his secret away! (21)
The image of the red Clydesider juggling or riding a
unicycle to entertain the weans on Buchanan Street is an
endearing one.

Yet MacLean was who he was. He inspires or frustrates us
because of the political animal that he was. This author
finds him quite inspiring. It would have been nice if he
had been at the Queens Park - Clyde game with his
daughters rather than the other side of Jordania at the
age of 44. This portrait has tried to bring the real
John MacLean through. The human being with the political
being; the social animal with the solitary one.

He was consistent and always principled. As he put it:

"The goal was to train and lead minds to break
capitalism and running the various national workers'
republics as a step forward to the ultimate goal, a
World Workers Republic. May Scotland keep in the van
with Wales and lead the Colonies and England into the
path of righteousness." (22)

To train and lead minds. Into the path of righteousness. John MacLean may have rejected religion and have always been a vocal critic of what he saw as the hypocrisy of organised religion. However, this is the boy who graduated from the Free Church speaking. There is no tongue in cheek. It is the language of religion applied to the real cause that he believed would free humanity. You cannot underestimate just how Presbyterian John MacLean was and the influence that religion had on him. If, as was said, Karl Kautsky was the "Pope of Marxism" then John MacLean was the Moderator of its Free Kirk General Assembly. As we have seen, Gael had a very high interest in ecclesiastical matters which may or may not have been shared by his readership. Indeed, I cannot think of any other Marxist who would give a report of the Free Church's General Assembly three years in a row! Gael would always take the line that he believed to be right, morally right, which meant that he was out of kilter with the mainstream long before he fell out with the Party in 1920.

This moralistic tone was adopted at various times in his speeches and writings. My personal favourite?

"Curse all charlatans who prevent the Salvation of Society." (23)

A bit of clichéd fire and brimstone and you may detect that socialist fire and brimstone jumping out of him throughout his life. He was referring to those who would delay progress in supporting the Irish cause and aiding the imperial ambitions of England and the US. He could, of course, have been referring to sinners in general. Many gloss over this part of MacLean's make up but it was essential to who he was and why he took some of the stances that he did because he believed that he was right. And it explains his lifelong fascination with the faith that he rejected and this is only natural as it played such a formative part in his early life.

John was a convert and he had the convert's enthusiasm to push and preach and persuade. His conversion from the

196

"cult of Christ" to a new cult of Marx is the starting point and end point of this portrait. This passion marked him out among his contemporaries and resonates today. What he wanted for Scotland, he wanted for the world and he summed it up in his last written words in his last election address that outlived him:

"Every vote cast for me is for world peace and eternal economic security for the human family." (24)

7 days later John MacLean found his own peace and eternal rest. He had truly given his life for this. Call it Social Democracy, call it Socialism or you can call it what you like! It is human just as Dubczek would describe it 45 years later. Hundreds sat in classrooms on Clydeside and beyond to listen to a Dominie preaching these values. If you believe in these values then find a new Dominie, buy her or him some chalk and an easel with a brief to teach us what we are trying to build and not just what we are out to replace and let's start all over again.

NOTES

1) Walt Whitman, Song of the Broad Axe, *Collected Poems*,

2) The Gospel of Luke, 21:14-15.,

3) Tom Anderson, Comrade John MacLean, MA, 1938, p. 46

4) John MacLean, "British Materialism and British Idealism", The Call, 23/2/1920. The article was a review of the Reverend Lee's pamphlet of the same name.

5) John MacLean Glasgow City Archive, Mitchell Library, TD260/29

6) Ibid, TD260/33

7) Dated 4/12/1923 and TD260/30 in the Archive

8) Dated 14/12/1923 and TD260/31

9) Ibid, TD260/34

10)   Tom Anderson commented that by 1930 Jean had still "stood aloof" from the Socialist movement.

11)   Glasgow Archive, TD260/28

12)   It is worth noting that in his Gael column many years earlier MacLean had paid tribute to a Doctor Devon as being socially aware on poverty. I don't know if it is the same one!

13)   Hamish Henderson, *The John MacLean March* in TS Law and Thurso Berwick, *Homage to John MacLean*, 1973, p. 11

14)   Law and Berwick, ibid, p. 3

15)   Tom Scott, *Til John MacLean*, in Law and Berwick, ibid. p. 28

16)   Neal Ascherson, *John MacLean: His sacrifice does not make him our Redeemer*, The Scotsman, 24/8/1979

17)   Gerard Cairns, Saturday Essay, The Herald, 28/11/1998

18)   James Hunter, The Gaelic Connection: The Highlands, Ireland and nationalism, 1873 – 1922, Scottish Historical Review, Vol 54, 1975.

19)   John MacLean, Supplement, The Socialist, December 1922.

20)   Rosa Luxemburg Speaks, 1986 edition, p.335

21)   Ibid. TD260/15for both letters. The letter to
   Lizzie is dated 28/6/1921.
22)   John MacLean, The Clyde and the general
   election, Supplement, The Socialist, December
   1922.
23)   John MacLean, The Irish Tragedy, Vanguard,
   November 1920
24)   John MacLean, General Election Address,
   Gorbals, 23 November 1923 in The Rapids, 1978, p.
   248.

Bibliography

Newspapers/Journals

Chapman

Guth na Bliadhna

History Ireland

Justice

Labour Review

Liberty - The Scottish Home Rule Journal

Scottish Historical Review

Scottish Workers Republic

Stornoway Gazette

Sunday Herald

Sunday Times Magazine

The Evening Times

The Herald

The Scotsman

The Scottish Review

The Socialist

The Vanguard

The Word

West Highland Free Press

Writings/Papers

John MacLean, *In The Rapids of Revolution*, 1978

MacLean Papers, National Library of Scotland, Edinburgh, Acc 4251

John MacLean Criminal Papers, Public Records Office, Edinburgh.

John MacLean Papers, Mitchell Library, Glasgow, TD260

MacLean Papers, Willie Gallacher Memorial Library, Glasgow Caledonian University

Biographies

Guy Aldred, *John MacLean - Martyr of the Class Struggle*, nd

Tom Anderson, *Comrade John*, 1930 and 1938

Graham Bain, *John MacLean: His Life and Work, 1918 - 1923* (pamphlet, nd)

Tom Bell, *John MacLean: A Fighter for Freedom*, 1944

John Broom, *John MacLean*, 1973

Nan Milton, *John MacLean*, 1973

B J Ripley and J McHugh, *John MacLean*, 1989.

Dave Sherry, *John MacLean: Red Clydesider*, 2014 edition

James D Young, *John MacLean: Clydeside Socialist*, 2000

Books

Freddy Anderson, *Krassivy - A Play about the great Socialist, John MacLean*, 2005

Terry Brotherstone (ed), *Covenant, Charter and Party - Traditions of revolt and protest in modern Scottish history*, 1989

Gordon Brown, *Maxton*, 1988

John Burrowes, *Irish: The Remarkable Saga of a Nation and a City*, 2004

Angus Calder, *Revolving Culture - Notes from the Scottish Republic*, 1994

John Taylor Caldwell, *Come Dungeons Dark - The life and times of Guy Aldred, Glasgow Anarchist*, 1988

Ewen A. Cameron, *Land for the People? The British Government and the Scottish Highlands, c 1880 - 1925*, 1996

Max Caulfield, *The Easter Rebellion*, Kindle edition, nd

Stuart Christie, *Granny made me an Anarchist*, 2004

Stephen Coyle, *High Noon on High Street*, 2008

Tony Dickson (ed), *Scottish Capitalism - Class, State and Nation from before the Union to the Present*, 1980

I Donnachie and G Hewitt, *Dictionary of Scottish History*, 2001

I Donnachie, C Harvie and I S Wood, *Forward! Labour Politics in Scotland, 1888 - 1988*, 1989

R Duncan and A McIvor, *Militant Workers - Labour and Class conflict on the Clyde 1900 - 1950, Essays in honour of Harry McShane*, 1992

R M Fox, *The History of the Irish Citizen Army*, 1944

Iain Frisor Grigor, *Highland Resistance: the Radical Tradition in the Scottish North*, 2000

Willie Gallacher, *Revolt on the Clyde*, 1936

Tom Gallagher, *Glasgow: The Uneasy Peace*, 1987

Donny Gluckstein, *The Western Soviets: Workers' Councils versus Parliament, 1915 - 1920*, 1985

Good News Bible, 1979

John Gray, *City in Revolt: James Larkin and the Belfast Dock Strike of 1907*,

C Desmond Greaves, *The Life and Times of James Connolly*, 1986 edition

Élie Halévy, *The Era of Tyrannies. Essay on Socialism and War*, 1967

Christopher Harvie, *Scotland and Nationalism*, 1977

David Hogan, *The Four Glorious Years*, 1953

David Howell, *A Lost Left: Three Studies in Socialism and Nationalism*, 1986

James Hunter, *The Last of the Free: A history of the Highlands and Islands of Scotland*, 1999

Walter Kendall, *The Revolutionary Movement in Britain, 1900 - 21*, 1969

William Knox (ed) *Scottish Labour Leaders, 1918 - 39*, 1984

V I Lenin, *Selected Works*, 1977

Rosa Luxemburg Speaks, 1986

A McCombes and R Paterson, *Restless Land: A Radical Journey through Scotland's history, Volume 1 (500AD - 1914)*, 2014

Hugh MacDiarmid, *A Drunk Man looks at the Thistle*, 1987 (edited by Kenneth Buthlay)

Ian MacDougall, *Voices from the Hunger Marches, Volume 1*, 1990

Iain McLean, *The Legend of Red Clydeside*, 1983

Karl Marx, *Capital*, Volume 1, 1954 edition

Marx - Engels Reader, 1981

Marx - Engels, *Selected Works in One Volume*, 1980 edition

Marx - Engels, *Ireland and the Irish Question*, 1988 edition

Robert K Middlemas, *The Clydesiders - A Left Wing Struggle for Parliamentary Power*, 1965

Robert K Middlemas, *Politics in Industrial Society*, 1979?

Edwin Muir, *Scottish Journey*, 1935

Máirtín Seán Ó Catháin, Irish Republicanism in Scotland, 1858 - 1916: Fenians in Exile, 2007

Ruán O'Donnell, *Patrick Pearse*, 2016

Murray Pittock, *A New History of Scotland*, 2003

H Savage and L Forster, *All for the Cause - Willie Nairn, 1856 - 1902: Stonebreaker, Philosopher, Marxist.* nd

Victor Serge, *Birth of Our Power*, 1931

T Sheridan and A McCombes, *Imagine: A Socialist Vision for the 21st Century*, 2000

John Slatter (ed) *From the Other Shore: Russian Political Emigrants in Britain, 1880-1917*, 1984

Angela Tuckett, *The Scottish Trades Union Congress: the First 80 Years, 1897 - 1977*, 1986

Mihaly Vajda, *The State and Socialism - Political Essays*, 1981

Graham Walker, *Intimate Strangers: Political and Cultural Interaction between Scotland and Ulster in modern times*, 1995

Walt Whitman, *Collected Poems*, nd

Barbara Winslow, *Sylvia Pankhurst*, 1996

James D Young, *The Rousing of the Scottish Working Class*, 1979

James D Young, *The Very Bastards of Creation: Scottish International Radicalism 1707 - 1995. A Biographical Study*, 1995

Articles

Neal Ascherson, *John MacLean: His Sacrifice does not make him our Redeemer*, Scotsman, 24/8/1979

Gerry Cairns, *John MacLean, Socialism and the Scottish Question*, Scottish Labour History Magazine, Autumn, 1989.

Gerry Cairns, Why John MacLean did not join the Communist Party of Great Britain, Scottish Workers Republic, An t-Earrach/Spring, 2005

Angus Calder, *The Leader of the Glasgow Soviet*, Sunday Times magazine, 25/11/1973

Gavin Foster, *Scotsmen, Stand by Ireland: John MacLean and the Irish Revolution*, History Ireland, Jan/Feb 2008

James Hunter, *The Gaelic Connection: the Highlands, Ireland and nationalism, 1873 - 1922*, Scottish Historical Review, Vol 54, 1975

Nan Milton, *John MacLean and Ireland*, Socialist Scotland/Alba Soisealach, Winter/Geamhradh, 1979

Ian Mitchell, *A Bolshevik's Visit to Lewis between the Wars,* West Highland Free Press, 20/9/1995

Academic Papers/Theses

David Burke, *Theodore Rothstein and Russian Political Émigré Influence on the British Labour Movement, 1884 - 1920*, Greenwich University thesis, 1997

James D Young, *Clydeside Socialism, May Day and the Second International*, International Conference of the Historians of the Labour Movement, September 1989

James D Young, *A Very English Socialism and the Celtic Fringe, 1880 - 1911*, John Hewitt Summer School, 1991

Pamphlets

Donald Anderson, *Scotland's Socialist Saint*, nd

Thiurso Berwick and T S Law, *Homage to John MacLean*, 1979

Terry Brotherstone (ed), *The Accuser of Capitalism: John MacLean's speech from the Dock, 9th May 1918*, 1986

John MacLean, *Lectures on Economics, 1979 (John MacLean Society)*

Harry McShane, Remembering John MacLean, 1979

Nan Milton, *John MacLean and Scottish Independence*, 1979

James D Young, John MacLean - Educator of the Working Class, 1991

Websites

Scottish Republican Socialist Movement

Marxists.org